Talking
Green

Talking Green

Colin Ward

Five Leaves Publications
www.fiveleaves.co.uk

Talking Green
by Colin Ward

Published in 2012
by Five Leaves Publications,
PO Box 8786, Nottingham NG1 9AW
www.fiveleaves.co.uk

ISBN 978-1907869518

Five Leaves acknowledges
financial support from
Arts Council England

Five Leaves is represented
to the trade by Turnaround
and distributed by Central Books

Typeset and designed by Four Sheets Design and Print
Printed by Imprint Digital in Exeter

Contents

Introduction

Talking Schools, Talking Houses, Talking to Architects...
all the subjects of previous sets of lectures by Colin Ward.
His interests were far wider than these concerns. Our
own firm alone has published books by him, sometimes
with others, on squatting, allotments, the plotlands of the
south of England, British holiday camps and anarchism.
For various reasons a planned set of lectures on green
issues was never published during his lifetime, but we
are glad to rectify that omission now.

Since his death in 2010 other books to do with Colin
Ward's work have appeared, including a Reader,
collecting extracts from writing across his range of interests, and a special issue of *Anarchist Studies*. There has
been a conference on childhood, the papers of which
should soon be published. Underpinning so much of his
work, however, were what could loosely be called green
concerns, some of which are represented here.

Several of the essays draw on his past books or
prefigure books which were yet to be written when he
gave the lectures. Colin Ward was a very popular visiting
lecturer as evidenced by the range of venues for the talks
in this collection – academic conferences, a local archaeological society, an occupation of unused land... it was all
one to him. All the talks were of course tailored to his
audiences, but, true to his green principles, he did a fair
amount of recycling, so some of his examples crop up in
more than one essay. That's not a bad thing. We have left
the lectures more or less as they were when given, save
for adding some references and citing later editions of
some of the books mentioned. Naturally some organisations have folded, government departments have changed
their names a time or two and had the lectures been
given later other examples might have been more appo-
site. Some things have changed for the worse, such as the

current government's plan to criminalise squatting, while generally green concerns have become more publicly acceptable. Nevertheless, all the lectures are worth reading, for their historic and contemporary interest.

I am grateful to Harriet Ward and Ben Ward for tracing a range of essays and working out which best represented Colin "talking green".

Ross Bradshaw
Five Leaves Publications
September 2012

A Doomwatch for the Pollution of our Land

Lecture at the Annual Conference of the Royal Society of Health, Eastbourne, April 1972, published in the *RSH Journal* Vol 92 No 4, August 1972.

This subject was originally intended to be discussed by Dr Kit Pedler, the man who conceived the television 'Doomwatch' series.* He is unfortunately unable to do this having been called abroad. Some people would be happy to see the last of him (they will be disappointed: another series has begun) because it is already fashionable to deplore the 'Doomwatch' approach to environmental health issues. I sometimes think that what they really dislike is the idea that every Tom, Dick and Harry in the mass television audience should have these topics dished out in dramatised form. There is always the danger that the public might really get interested. Better leave it to the experts. This point of view was made explicitly by the Chief Alkali Inspector. "What evidence have you got for public concern?" he asked Jon Tinker, Environment Consultant of the *New Scientist*. "A lot of this trouble is caused by one or two militants and agitators. The general public doesn't give a damn about figures."[1]

On the other hand, the kind of environmental hazard that is dramatised by 'Doomwatch' is so infinitely more worth ventilating in public than the usual fare of television drama, that people with a professional concern should welcome its presentation to a mass audience. What *I* dislike intensely is the formula of the dramas in

---

Doomwatch ran on BBC television between 1970 and 1972. It featured fictional stories on environmental issues.

which the all-wise Dr Quist, with his direct line to Downing Street, is the man on whose broad shoulders our fragile hopes of continued existence are laid. He is a kind of Perry Mason, Dr Who and Chairman Mao all rolled into one, solving *our* problems for us. The secret life of Walter Mitty, Public Health Inspector. Whereas in real life, as we know all too well, the battle for environmental health is fought by thousands of real public health inspectors, medical officers, pollution officers, and officials of local and central government high and low, all of them subject to the constraints that a rigidly hierarchical and paternalistic public service tradition involves, together with that minority of the general public which feels a concern for one or other of the issues involved. All of them fallible, few of them powerful, and all operating in a densely-populated country which, economically and socially, has higher priorities than the health of our environment.

No one would suggest that the 'Doomwatch' plays are great or immortal works of art, but there does exist one great drama which is absolutely relevant to this topic. This is Ibsen's *An Enemy of the People,* which in its original published version is entitled *A Doomwatch for Environmental Pollution (a) Pollution of Land — An Enemy of the People.* I have dragged it into the title of this paper, even though it is the 'Medical Officer of Health', rather than the pollution he exposes, to whom Ibsen sardonically gives *his* title. His hero, Dr Stockmann, is medical officer to the public baths which are the pride of the town and the source of prosperity because of the tourist trade they bring. Puzzled by cases of typhoid and gastric fever, Dr Stockmann sends samples of both drinking water and sea water to the university for chemical analysis, and the report reveals that the water is full of putrified organic matter. The Board suppresses his report, the local paper is influenced to refuse the account he wrote for publication. In desperation he calls a public meeting to hear his testimony, but the meeting

10

passes a resolution that the Medical Officer is an enemy of the people, and he is threatened with prosecution if he reveals in writing that the source of contamination is the tannery of a local industrialist. Even his daughter is obliged to quit her teaching job, and his boys are suspended from the grammar school. In the last scene he is planning to start a school himself for the local guttersnipes, in the hope of rearing a few decent and independent-minded citizens.

Let us hope that the same thing would not happen to anybody who revealed some of the uncomfortable truths about pollution which they come across in the exercise of their duties, but to quote again from Jon Tinker's investigation, "If a factory-owner should choose to pour thousands of gallons of cyanide into a river, the maximum fine the courts can impose is £100. But if a river inspector analyses a sample of this effluent, and mentions the results to a member of the public, he can be sent to prison for three months. Far too often the Prevention of Pollution Acts function as Acts for the Protection of Polluters." He was writing a couple of months ago, and the first of the penalties, thanks to recent publicity about the scandal of cyanide dumping, will soon be very considerably increased. But what about the second? Will it remain? And why? Mr. Tinker remarks that "this mania for preserving industrial secrecy at the expense of public participation and at the risk of public safety runs right through British pollution law and procedure." While to get back to Dr Stockmann's dilemma, Kenneth Tyler of the Association of Public Health Inspectors told Mr Tinker that "an inspector would be a very unwise man if he started releasing details of individual discharges to sewers." Ibsen's play, by the way, was written ninety years ago.

From the point of view of building up an informed public opinion about pollution, this 'Nanny Knows Best' approach is absolutely to be condemned. One of the few things that crosses the gap between staid and solid

11

public officials and the disaffected radical young, is a concern with the pollution of the environment. The young have a moral concern about these issues. One has only to read the so-called 'underground' press to see this, or to talk to the Conservation Officer of the National Union of Students. (How many other unions employ one?) It is felt at the school level too. I receive dozens of letters a week from boys and girls and teachers wanting sources of information on one topic or other relating to the pollution of the environment. The Water Pollution Research Laboratory had over five hundred requests from schools for advice on pollution projects during the period covered by its last annual report, and its Director of Research remarks that a few years ago even one would have seemed unusual. The Northcott Theatre, Exeter, puts on an annual show for Devon schools, and asking for a theme for last year's performance, was told on all sides, "Make it about pollution." It would certainly be sad if the restraints of a misplaced sense of discretion were to make the public officials seem to be covering up for the polluters rather than to be welcoming energetic young allies in the struggle to change our habits as a nation.

Dr Pedler, several years ago, made what I thought to be a highly significant remark: "I very strongly believe that there should be some sort of real-life equivalent to 'Doomwatch'. Not acting for the Government, but investigating on behalf of *the people.*" [2] Now, investigating on behalf of the people is exactly what the professionals of the pollution-monitoring services are supposed to be doing. As their lips seem to be sealed, the growth of independent environment watchdogs in university departments is not only what might be expected but is very much to be welcomed, and the story of the involvement of the University of Bristol's Sabrina project in the Rio Tinto Zinc smelter at Avonmouth indicates how very much in the public interest this independent involvement can be. The same may turn out to be true of the work of students of the

Open University, and that done by students of the post-graduate MSc course on environmental pollution at Leeds.

Dr Kenneth Mellanby's warnings at the British Association's Swansea meeting last year, that Government departments were censoring scientific results, not because national or commercial security was involved, but because they were embarrassing, drew attention to the need for *someone* to say embarrassing things.

> Only university scientists retain the right to publish what they see fit, and even then their right is sometimes curtailed. There is, for example, a growing amount of research in university departments sponsored by industry and subject to commercial security. So for a majority of scientists the right to publish is very far from absolute. Their primary loyalties are not to some abstract idea of science but to their employers.[3]

This is true of civil servants. One assumes that it is true of local government officers, though so far as is known it is not written into any contract they may sign. We are still in the Stockmann situation:

> *Mayor:* I must insist most emphatically that all matters be considered and dealt with through the proper channels and by the appropriate authorities. I cannot permit any dubious or underhand methods.
>
> *Dr Stockmann:* Since when have I used dubious or underhand methods?
>
> *Mayor:* You have a chronic disposition to take things into your own hands, at least. And in a well-ordered community, that can be equally reprehensive. The individual must be ready to subordinate himself to the community as a whole; or, more precisely, to the authorities charged with the welfare of that community.[4]

Dr Stockmann's dilemma (though as a simple and upright man *he* didn't see that he had a problem) is one which affects all the environmental professions. Some

13

members of some of them have made an attempt to face squarely the question of where their loyalties lie. The Institution of Municipal Engineers in its recent statement on Environmental Pollution declared:

> Members of the Institution cannot and would not wish to dissociate themselves from the heavy responsibilities of scientists and technologists, who are ultimately both the originators of pollution and its only destroyers and without whom no improvement or development of the environment would be possible. Through its commitment to public service, the Institution stands on the progressive side, and is happily freed from most of the strong contrary influences.[5]

It is only when one gets down to specific cases that the difficulties arise. I assume that when the urban motorway known as Westway was built in London, its creators were fully paid-up members of the Institution of Municipal Engineers. But in all the years when the scheme was in preparation, did one of them inquire what was to happen to the tenants of Acklam Road, North Kensington, when the motorway destroyed their environment without actually eliminating their homes? Only the militant protests of the tenants themselves brought them the promise of rehousing. Now the highway engineer would of course say, "But this is not within our competence. It is a matter for the Housing Department." The same kind of awkward problem arises in most environmental situations. Whatever happens, and whatever decision is taken, someone gets hurt, and it is usually the people who are least able to speak up for themselves, or are least informed about what is going to hit them, who are most vulnerable.

One minority group of professional local government officers have been struggling to define their role in a way which attempts to link it with the community outside the town hall. These are the handful of planners who publish the journal *Community Action*. An article there defines three roles for the planner:

a. 'The Expert' or 'The Technician': Planners as scientific experts proposing solutions or giving advice independent of the political process because they possess a particular and specialised knowledge.

b. 'The Bureaucrat': Planners as the agents of their political masters (like local councillors) proposing solutions which fit the requirements of the ruling parties.

c. 'The Advocate': Planners as the agents of particular powerless or underprivileged groups or communities, proposing solutions which fit their needs and requirements.[6]

The authors reject the role of "experts" because of the value assumptions necessary in any process of design policies. (In the instance I mentioned above, the value assumption was that rapid private transport for the out-of-town commuter or the commercial vehicle was more valuable than the environment of the inhabitants of North Kensington.) They therefore recommend a marriage of the role of "The Bureaucrat" with that of "The Advocate" and invent for this new role the name of "The Bureaucratic Guerilla":

> A guerilla harasses an army in small bands. This reflects in reality the limited number of planners in local government who presently adopt this role. The term 'The Bureaucratic Guerilla' is used to describe a role for planners working for local government bureaucracies where their ends are different from and in conflict with those of their employers.

They go on to spell out the implications of adopting this role: "technical assistance to particular groups and communities; provision of information which is available but not necessarily accessible to particular groups and communities; provision of information which is *not* normally available; provision of knowledge of the most effective ways of using the local government system to achieve more resources for a particular group of community," and so on.

These radical planners, faced with Dr Stockmann's dilemma, have chosen to be what Ralph Nader called "whistle-blowers", and to break with the vow of silence or the conspiracy of silence that keeps the public and the press out of key meetings, and maintains that all must be for the best. "I consider it imperative," says the Mayor in Ibsen's play, "that your report should not be presented to the Board. In the public interest, it must be withheld." *We* consider it imperative, say the bureaucratic guerillas, that the people affected by this or that proposal shall be told of it and how to fight it.

Ralph Nader claims that:

> We've got to develop an ethic of whistle-blowing. We've got to develop a kind of common law of whistle-blowing, with a principle [sic] responsibility of the professional society to take this on as a major mission. Not that it is going to justify every whistle-blower, but that it's going to basically inquire into such cases and to see if there was due process and fair treatment and to try to generate a freer climate within these organisations that will encourage dissent and internal criticisms, internal self-examinations. It is the lack of all these traits that leads to our hand-wringing about bureaucratic inadequacy, fossilisation, non-responsiveness, stick-in-the-mudism, and the like.[7]

But perhaps we haven't got to worry about anybody blowing the whistle. There were no whistles blowing in the case of Rio Tinto Zinc at Avonmouth, nor at the United Carbon Black factory in the Port Tennant district of Swansea. There it was the residents' blockade of the factory which called the bluff of official concern over pollution. As one resident remarked,

> I remember picking water lilies, wild irises, bulrushes and blackberries from the banks of the canal. As children we swam there. There were swans and we held fishing competitions. Now we have to wash our windows every

day, spend at least 75p a week on a family wash at the launderette and dare not put a baby in its pram in the garden. All this when everybody's talking about pollution and conservation.[8]

This instance reminds us that though the theme of this paper is supposed to be the pollution of the land, this is inseperable from that of the air and water which are the themes of other papers. I have a friend who is so out of touch with economic realities that he grows vegetables for the market without the use of inorganic fertilisers and pesticides. But *his* land and *his* water and his crops are polluted in his opinion by the use of his prairie-farming neighbours in Suffolk of these substances sprayed from an aeroplane. What redress has he? If he complains people think him mad: all those free chemicals falling like manna on his hungry land.

But whatever kind of pollution is being considered, my plea is that we drop the gentleman's agreement to say and do nothing that might offend someone, or harm the vested interests of the rich and powerful. I was privileged to hear last November the New York Environmental Protection Administrator, Jerome Kretchmer, describing the insoluble problems of that city and declaring that "Even allowing for considerable differences in national attitudes, I suggest to you that New York's problems await *you,* just around the corner." *The Times* described him as "Angry, fighting, aggressive and outspoken" and remarked that "In Britain we have yet to meet anyone like Mr Kretchmer in the administration." Well, everyone might feel a lot happier if they had. Mr Kretchmer was not mealy-mouthed about naming names. "We have seen the enemy," he said, "and it is General Motors." As he described his city's problems of water supply, sewerage, refuse disposal, traffic congestion and atmospheric pollution, he had to confess that his solitary success was in the latter field, and he attributed such advances as had been made to his habit of making public announcements

17

that "This is an Unsafe Day" and allowing the public to note the frequency of such announcements.

> The real estate industry almost single-handedly tied up a crucially important air control law in the courts; the container industries, working behind the scenes, managed to emasculate the recycling incentive tax; merchants blindly opposed experimental street closings, although data showed sales were not adversely affected; an extraordinary array of Chambers of Commerce and city-wide business associations pressured the New York Mayor, John V. Lindsay, unsuccessfully, in an attempt to kill the new air code, charging that it was 'hastily drawn up' when in fact it was badly needed and had been painstakingly prepared for some ten months.[9]

Mr. Kretchmer thought that as public awareness of the environmental crisis of American cities grows in the next few years, a "neo-populist" alliance between the environmental professions and the consumer protection movement was likely to come into being. "We are far more likely to see some harsh struggles than early and easy accommodations." I would like to see local health authorities emerge from the anonymity of discreet silent watchdogs in the Town Hall, to become outspoken public crusaders for the protection of the environment. I mentioned earlier Ralph Nader's call for "Whistle-blowing". He was defining the responsibilities of a profession, and he said:

> The words *professionalism* and *professional society* are bandied about often without definition because the definition is very uncomfortable. I think one try at that would define a profession, in contradiction to a trade, as a body of learned knowledge with an ability to self-examine itself and its purposes; an ability to link its body of knowledge with other bodies of knowledge to achieve common purposes; the ability to defend dissent, not just within the society but dissent by its members in conflicts with their employer organisations or their government agencies or corporations; and above all the ability to pioneer new policies that are not brought into effect by market incentives.[10]

He charged the professions with failing to live up to these responsibilities. The realities, he said, were first that the professions "tend to be indentured to the particular corporations or industries that deal with their subject matter, second that they don't defend the whistle-blower, and thirdly that they have an almost irresistible impulse to plunge to lowest common denominators." Are we confident that this is untrue of the environmental professions in this country today? Nader charged the environmental professions in the United States with ignoring "virulent environmental violence." And he went on to define this in these terms:

> The problem of environmental violence is one which should be a major subject of focus because even to this day, I think we will have to admit, pollution is still considered by most people as something that is foul smelling or evil or ugly-looking and is not considered as perhaps one of two of the most domestically-virulent forms of violence in our society, the other being traffic crashes. Street crime, burglaries, campus disruptions, don't amount to a fingernail's proportion of the destruction of human beings and their health and their property from traffic crashes and environmental contamination.[11]

Though we are gradually coming round to the principle that "the polluter must pay" — a point which seems elementary enough — we have hardly begun to see the polluter as criminal, and we are still far from the idea that those with power and authority can be accessories after the fact. Peter Hoefnagels, Professor of Criminology at Rotterdam, wrote a pamphlet called *On the Crime of Destroying the Viability of the Environment* and his students are staging a trial this month of the Aldermen and Officers of the City of Rotterdam charging them with this crime. It is gratifying to note that these people have agreed to appear as defendants. This public dramatisation of environmental issues is going to add immensely to public awareness and public action. But can anyone imagine in Britain, the councillors and their officers agreeing to take part in what they would no doubt call a charade? As it is, the secretiveness of local authorities is still such that only one in ten open all their committees to the press and half open none.[12]

Within the structure of a large authority the planning officer, the engineer and the housing manager may have quite different priorities, aims and objectives; there may be a struggle which ordinary citizens don't know about and consequently can't take sides in for the influence or the control of policy between different officers or between their different committees. Who decides? When the same officer is the overlord for all three functions, which weighs most heavily in his judgement and in the recommendations that he makes to his council? The reason for asking this question is because it has every relevance to the pollution of our land. No-one will disagree with me that the worst pollutant of the environment is the internal combustion engine. There is not only the air pollution it causes, nor the death and mutilation that is taken for granted as a by-product. There is especially the way in which the insistence on getting motor vehicles into the heart of our pre-motor age cities is destroying them as habitable places, making vast areas of no man's land, turning the city into a place which is not fit for humans and certainly not for their children, and even killing off alternate and more rational means of transportation by destroying their economic feasibility.

Someone must have staked his professional reputation on getting the traffic through. But listen to this description of the motor car:

It is probably the most wasteful and uneconomic contrivance which has yet appeared among our personal possessions. The average passenger load of motor cars in our streets is certainly less than two persons and in terms of transportable load some 400 cu.ft. of vehicle weighing over 1 ton is used to convey 4 cu.ft. of humanity

> weighing about 2 cwt., the ratios being about 10 to 1 in
> weight and 100 to 1 in bulk. The economic implication of
> this situation is ridiculous and I cannot believe it to be
> permanent.[13]

Now who said that ? It was actually Sir Herbert Manzoni, the former City Engineer for Birmingham whose legacy to that city, at enormous expense, has been to carve the heart out of it to get the traffic through. Sir Herbert on his own testimony didn't "believe" in the motor car as a permanent aspect of the city scene but felt obliged to fulfil his duty and make a city where cars are more important than people. This is appeasing the polluter with a vengeance, and it is done presumably on the principle that the motoring lobby must at all costs be served. Other cities are in the process of doing what Birmingham has done, though scarcely with such singleminded determination. Leeds is at least learning to give priority to the pedestrian, London at stupefying cost is committed to a disastrous urban motorway policy, in the next stage of which a block of flats that I worked on ten years ago will have the motorway at fourth-floor level perhaps only 15 feet away. But when I talk to municipal officials I find them as individuals just as horrified by the juggernaut of destruction and pollution which urban motorways bring to our cities. It is not a political matter in party terms; elections come and go with changes in the councils but the policies go on.

Yet if *one* city's officers were to produce a scheme for a car-free centre, with alternatives like free or flat central area public transport, as a working model for the task which all must undertake sooner or later, they would go down in history as the saviours of the urban environment. Our grandchildren will look back on the motor age as a twentieth century aberration, and will wonder why we ever conceived that universal motoring was a step forward in human freedom when it will be so obvious to them that it was our most deadly pollutant.

They will wonder too why we allowed manufacturers to inflict indestructible packaging upon us, while contributing nothing towards the cost of disposal. They will wonder what kind of vandals we were as private citizens in treating the whole country as one vast rubbish dump. But they will wonder most of all why those who accepted a professional responsibility for safeguarding the environment did not shout long and loud that our social and economic priorities prevented them from fulfilling their tasks.

To sum up: the point that I want to make is that it is time for the environmental protection services to emerge from their anonymous self-effacing role of silent servants in the town hall, into the "angry, fighting, aggressive and outspoken" stance of someone like Mr Kretchmer in New York. And if we take the question of pollution seriously, this means the highway engineer abandoning the philosophy of getting the traffic through at all costs to one of keeping the city habitable at all costs, it means the inspectorate, whether the P.H.I., the Alkali Inspector, or the River Board, dropping the ethic of secrecy for one of open diplomacy, it means loud, tough talking about the menace of over-packaging and non-destructible packaging materials, it means all authorities adopting biologically sane sewage disposal systems — which some already do — a task which will take decades and cost a fortune.

It means a philosophy of recycling in refuse disposal, again at enormous cost. It means ramming home to citizens that the polluter must pay.

Dr Stockmann, in *An Enemy of The People,* told his fellow townsmen that he had discovered something "incomparably bigger than this petty business about the water-supply being polluted and the Baths standing over a cesspool."

"We don't want to hear about that," said his audience. But the M.O.H. went on to reveal his discovery "that all our *spiritual* sources are polluted and that our whole civic community is built over a cesspool of lies."

There is no need to go as far as that, but all the environmental protection services have a duty to point out to the citizens, whether manufacturer, retailer, motorist or householder, that in exercising their freedom to produce and consume how they like, and to travel how they like, they are fouling their own nest and destroying their own habitat.

References

1   Jon Tinker: 'Britain's Environment — Nanny knows best', *New Scientist,* 9 March 1972, pp. 530-534.
2   Kit Pedler, interviewed in *Radio Times,* 10 December 1970.
3   Bryan Silcock: 'Why are these Scientists Muzzled?', *Sunday Times,* 12 September 1971.
4   Ibsen: *An Enemy of the People,* trans. by James Walter McFarlane (Vol. VI of the Oxford Ibsen [O.U.P., 1960]).
5   *Journal of the Institution of Municipal Engineers,* January 1972.
6   'Bureaucratic Guerilla: an alternative role for the local authority planner' *Community Action,* No. 1, Feb. 1972.
7   Ralph Nader: 'The Professional Responsibilities of a Professional Society', *American Institute of Planners Newsletter,* Vol. 5, No. 11, November 1970.
8   *Peace News,* 9 July, 1971.
9   *The Surveyor,* 26 November 1971.
10   Ralph Nader, *op. cit.*
11   Ralph Nader, *op. cit.*
12   *Admission of the Press to Committee Meetings* (Institute of Public Relations, 1972).
13   Sir Herbert J. Manzoni: Paper read at the R.I.B.A., 21 Jan. 1958 *(R.I.B.A. Journal,* March 1958).

The Urban Predicament

Paper given at the conference on the Human Habitat at the Royal Institution, London, March 1975

In natural environments, there are rich ecological systems where an equilibrium has evolved between different varieties of flora and fauna, each flourishing, with a specific relationship with the others, at their own level. In the modern rural environment, of course, especially in districts devoted to grain production, this variety has been systematically reduced. The systematic removal of hedges, trees, the drainage of ponds and the elimination of patches of uncultivated land, as well as the use and abuse of pesticides and of nitrogenous fertilisers which of course find their way into ditches, streams and rivers, has coarsened this finely-textured variety of species, producing an attenuated environment.

In terms of human ecology, the traditional rural environment is not rich. (Today it is even less so, as the charming old cottages fill up with weekending urban dwellers, while the peasants commute from their council houses to the nearest town.) It is the variety of human activities, human contacts and human opportunities, which have been the magnet drawing people towards the city. Whenever there was an opportunity of gaining a foothold in the urban economy (and even when, as in many of the exploding cities of the Third World today, the opportunity is often an illusion) people drifted to the city.

What did they seek? A chance to meet more people. More kinds of entertainment. Better chances for their children. A bigger choice of things to buy. A better place to live. The excitement and stimulus of a place where there is always something happening (instead of what

24

Karl Marx curtly called the "idiocy of rural life"), and above all a greater choice and range of jobs.

History is full of evocations of the wonder and incredible drama of the city, where the streets are paved with gold, where every whim and fancy can be satisfied (if you can afford it), where you are free from the censorious eyes and the same old faces of the small town; it's the place where opportunity knocks.

Our contemporary image of the city is not like this. The very title of this conference — the urban predicament — indicates that we see the city not as a wonderland, but as an environmental disaster. An American friend of mine, Murray Bookchin, writing of the cities of the United States, says in his book *The Limits of the City:*

> They are disintegrating administratively, institutionally, and logistically; they are increasingly unable to provide the minimal services for human habitation, personal safety, and the means of transporting people and goods..." Even, he remarks, where cities have some semblance of formal democracy, "almost every civic problem is resolved not by action that goes to its social roots, but by legislation that further restricts the rights of the citizen as an autonomous being and enhances the power of super-individual agencies.

He is profoundly sceptical about the impact of the environmental professions on the city, and reminds us that "Not surprisingly, some of the most humanist notions of urbanism come from amateurs who retain contact with the authentic experiences of people and the mundane agonies of metropolitan life." In a British context this is certainly true: the most creative stream in town planning ideology stems from Ebenezer Howard who was a shorthand writer and Patrick Geddes who was a biologist. But the dominant stream, as it affects the inner city, stems from the Metropolitan Improvement and Public Health legislation of the 19th century, as well as from the unholy alliance in the last decade between planning authorities and speculative get-rich-quick urban pirates, in search of the maximum lettable floor space. This kind of planning has the same environmental crudifying and coarsening effect on the city as the modern cereal-production has had in the country. It has sought to make the crooked places straight, to iron out the kinks, to eliminate non-conforming users (the urban flora and fauna who impede profit-maximisation!) and, in short, to impose geometry upon urban geography.

There is of course a quieter, gentler and more responsive tradition which stems from the notions of "conservative surgery" preached and practised by Patrick Geddes, with the intention of combining the conservation of the whole with the renewal of parts in the urban environment, cherishing rather than eliminating the *genius loci*. It is gradually dawning on us that total renewal, with the years of dereliction, of demolition, of subsequent building operations — means that after a generation or two the *whole* environment becomes obsolete simultaneously, so that total destruction and replacement have to happen all over again. We are rapidly rediscovering this alternative tradition, partly because the bottom is said to have fallen out of the property market, and partly because the energy crisis is adding a new dimension — energy budgeting — to our assessment of urban futures.

But immense damage — environmentally — has already been done: it has brought a shift from a fine-grain to a coarse-grain environment. This is very obvious in the surface texture — the change from small-scale buildings with a lot of visual interest to large-scale buildings with much less to beguile the eye. The coarse, crude, slab-like character of post-war buildings slaps you in the face in every British city, from pavement to skyline.

It is also apparent in the economic and social pattern of the city. All those small-scale business enterprises which provided the enormous variety of service trades and occupations which are one of the reasons why people congregate in cities in the first place, disappear because the high rents of new buildings cannot be sustained by the turnover of small businesses depending on low overheads. No umbrella-repairers, picture-frame makers, pastrycooks or ballet-shoe makers. No voluntary organisations, small publishers or chiropodists. Only large-scale, highly capitalised, high-turnover and big-profit entrepreneurs need apply.

It affects the homeless too. The gradual disappearance of cheap rented accommodation, boarding houses and common lodging-houses, means that there is nowhere for the poor and homeless to lay their heads. This of course is one of the reasons for the growing 'problem' of homeless single people in the cities. There are more people sleeping rough in London today than in, for instance, New York, where there are still cheap, run-down properties, and consequently somewhere for people to sleep at all levels of wealth and poverty.

Similarly, this coarsening of the urban structure implies the death of cheap eating-houses and places of entertainment: no room for them in the new office blocks and shopping centres of the rebuilt city. The effect of this coarsening of the texture of urban life can be seen in every city of the country.

The new urban environment discriminates against the poor — that goes without saying. It discriminates against the old too — they are just a nuisance. As the German writer Alexander Mitscherlich says (he is talking about Munich, but it might as well be anywhere), it discriminates against the child: "The anthropologist cannot get over the fact that the commercially-oriented planning of our cities is clearly aimed at one age group only — working adults — and even then inadequately enough. How a child is to become a working adult seems to be a negligible factor. The world of the child is a sphere of the socially weak, and is ruthlessly manipulated."

The worst piece of advice that planners have ever accepted was Daniel Burnham's injunction to "Make no little plans". Regardless of the fact that the planning officer is often quite low in the pecking order in County and City Halls (even among the environmental professions — where others — the highway engineer, the director of housing and so on — may wield more effective power and influence). And regardless of the fact that we have consistently failed to solve the problem of land acquisition and of betterment values — upon which the effective use of the planning legislation we have depends — regardless of this, we have insisted on thinking big, and on drawing up plans which are totally unrealistic, or which depended upon the projection into the future of economic and demographic trends which have proved to be transient.

In a strange way, the poorest and most deprived cities, the ones with the greatest unemployment problems and the least resources for redevelopment, have been the ones most intent on obliterating their past. Writing about the dreadful plight of the city of Liverpool, the planner Mike Franks declares:

> For the last hundred years the men of the corporation, both political and technical, have run a closed shop in local government. Liverpudlians have long been actively denied the knowledge and learning they would have needed to have stood up to the brave new world plans of their leaders. The city council has treated them like children whose needs must be administered to and in doing so have created retarded adults uncertain whether to expect what they need or to go out and get it.

He thinks that the burgeoning of citizens' groups and community action associations, are the final turn of the work, and the only hope for the urban future.

The point that Mr Franks makes is valuable because it underlines something we seldom think about. The traditional city: its topographical, social and economic pattern was comprehensible to its inhabitants. They knew how it worked. The functions and the functioning of

28

the city were *transparent*. But in the central area redevelopments, the inner ring road-building, the out-of-town supermarket developments of the last two decades, our intuitions play us false. The alienation or anomie which some people find characteristic of modern city life, is certainly made manifest in the citizen's relationship to his environment.

Eric Midwinter, also from Liverpool — where he ran the Educational Priority Area project — noted this in referring to what he called the planner's lipservice to consultation. "They may," he said, "knock on the door of a client for rehabilitation or decantation, and ask what sort of home and environment is required. What is the unfortunate interviewee to say in answer to this? What, in too many cases, he could say is something like: 'I was never educated to listen to that kind of question nor to articulate responses, technical or creative, to it.'"

There is an urgent need to establish the principle of *Transparency of Operation* in the city. The professionals and their political masters have erected a great smokescreen of pseudo-science to keep the citizens out of environmental decision-making. In practice, fortunately, this is useless. Think of all those recent decisions, arrived at after employing every kind of fabulously expensive specialist wisdom, which have been overturned as a result of the opposition of groups of outraged citizens: in the metropolitan area alone, one could list the London motorway proposals, the siting of the third London airport, Covent Garden, and Piccadilly. What price expertise? The lesson is that the awareness and environmental sophistication of the ordinary citizen is much more important than the professional wisdom of the experts. Ivan Illich, probably the most damaging of the new critics of the professionalisation of knowledge, remarks that:

It makes people dependent on having their knowledge produced for them. It leads to a paralysis of the moral and political imagination. This cognitive disorder rests on the illusion that the knowledge of the individual citizen is of less value than the "knowledge" of science. The former is the opinion of individuals. This *is* merely subjective and is excluded from policies. The latter is "objective" — defined by science and promulgated by expert spokesmen. This objective knowledge is viewed as a commodity which can be refined, constantly improved, accumulated and fed into a process, now called "decision-making". This new mythology of governance by the manipulation of knowledge-stock inevitably erodes reliance on government by people... Overconfidence in "better knowledge" becomes a self-fulfilling prophecy. People first cease to trust their own judgement and then want to be told the truth about what they know. Overconfidence in "better decision-making" first hampers people's ability to decide for themselves and then undermines their belief that they can decide.

His view coincides with mine, and explains why I personally am involved in the environmental education business. I think that the role of environmental education is nothing less than that of education for mastery of the environment. (If it isn't, I can't imagine what it *is* for).

I would like in the first place to think of the challenge to our assumptions presented by those cities where rapid urbanisation is actually happening today. In the poor cities of the Third World, in the cities of Asia, Africa and Latin America, the enormous movement of population into the big cities during the last two decades has resulted in the growth of huge peripheral squatter settlements around the existing cities, inhabited by the 'invisible' people who have no official urban existence. The English architect Pat Crooke points out that cities grow and develop on two levels, the official theoretical level and the popular actual unofficial level, and that the majority of the population of many Latin American cities are unofficial citizens with a 'popular economy' outside the institutional financial structure of the city. The official view, from city officers, governments, newspaper-men and international agencies, is that such settlements are the breeding-grounds for every kind of crime, vice, disease, social and family disorganisation. How could they not be, since they sprang up without official sanction or finance and as the result of illegal seizure of land?

The reality is different. Another English architect, John Turner, says:

> Ten years of work in Peruvian *barriadas* indicates that such a view is grossly inaccurate: although it serves some vested political and bureaucratic interests, it bears little relation to reality... Instead of chaos and disorganisation, the evidence instead points to highly organised invasions of public land in the face of violent police opposition, internal political organisation with yearly local elections, thousands of people living together in an orderly fashion with no police protection or public services. The original straw houses constructed during the invasions are converted as rapidly as possible into brick and cement structures with an investment totalling millions of dollars in labour and materials. Employment rates, wages, literacy, and educational levels are all higher than in central city slums (from which more *barriada* residents have escaped) and higher than the national average. Crime, juvenile delinquency, prostitution, and gambling are rare, except for petty thievery, the incidence of which *is* seemingly smaller than in other parts of the city.

If you think that this is simply romanticising other people's poverty, I ought to remind you that the poor of a poor country in an inefficiently administered city like Lima have not been deprived of the last shred of personal autonomy and human dignity like the poor of a rich and competently administered city like London. And I wonder what the ILEA Chief Education Officer would say of a community of poor people who were not only prepared to provide the labour and materials to build their own schools, but were ready to hire their own teachers too?

Let me turn to a totally different aspect of the way the environmentalist looks at the city. The city makes fantastic demands on energy resources. I have not seen

31

any comparisons made, though someone somewhere must be making a comparison between the energy consumption of one large city and that of the same population dispersed in a different pattern of settlements. Certainly when we think of possible alternative sources of energy, the point was made, again by Murray Bookchin, long before the energy crisis hit people's consciousness. He remarked that:

> To maintain a large city requires immense quantities of coal and petroleum. By contrast, solar energy, wind power and tidal energy reach us mainly in small packets. Except for great dams and turbines, the new devices seldom provide more than a few thousand kilowatt-hours of electricity. It is hard to believe that we will ever be able to design solar collectors that can furnish us with the immense blocks of electric power produced by a giant steam plant; it is equally difficult to conceive of a battery of wind turbines that will provide us with enough electricity to illuminate Manhattan Island. If homes and factories are heavily concentrated, devices for using clean sources of energy will probably remain mere playthings; but if urban communities are reduced in size and widely spread over the land, there is no reason why these devices cannot be combined to provide us with all amenities of an industrial civilisation. To use solar, wind and tidal power effectively, the giant city must be dispersed. A new type of community, carefully tailored to the nature and resources of a region, must replace the sprawling urban belts of today.

Another kind of energy crisis of the modern metropolis is that of the human energy it needs to service it. Anti-metropolitan writers have always maintained that the big city is a drain on the resources of its hinterland. (Actually of course one could also argue that the commuting hinterland is a drain on the resources of the city, which services the commuters but receives no rate revenue from them.) But it is certainly true to say that every metropolis requires an army of poor and immobile inhabitants to maintain its essential services.

I never walk through the Bayswater/South Kensington districts of London without speculating on the size of the huge servant class of the Edwardian era. In the last half-century all those cooks, parlourmaids, valets and gentlemen's gentlemen voted with their feet out of personal service and into occupations where wages were better and where collective bargaining modified the capriciousness of individual employers. And the family? They sold the house for conversion into flats and moved into the coachman's cottage in the mews, cosily modernised with a labour-saving kitchen. More recently, of course, they have actually been able to buy personal service again and have a Portuguese cook and an au pair.

The more recent, and more serious, decline has been not in personal service but in public services. The bigger the city, the worse the problem: it has hit London and the conurbations far harder than small towns. We already have a foretaste of the future metropolis: London Transport services continually curtailed for lack of train and bus crews, part-time schooling for lack of teachers, an ever-declining postal service, uncollected refuse in dirty streets, vital functions like hospitals or fire brigades seriously understaffed. The deputy leader of the GLC declared that London is "a city in crisis" facing a breakdown of its public services. The same has long been true of New York.

Yet at the same time there is unemployment in the city, and again the crudely conceived policies of redevelopment are destroying that rich pattern of specialist labour-intensive occupations which were one of the reasons for the development of cities in the first place. The reason why many people, who couldn't care less about the architectural issues involved, are opposed to the redevelopment of the south-eastern sides of Trafalgar Square is that 180 small businesses would be killed off. In another part of central London, the Tolmers area near Euston, where there are rival redevelopers: private speculators and the Camden Council, the Tolmers Village

33

Association conducted a survey and found that there were 105 small businesses employing about 1,000 people, which would be obliged to close down, whichever scheme of redevelopment was adopted.

Seventy-five years ago Ebenezer Howard wrote his famous book *Garden Cities of Tomorrow*,[2] which eventually led to the New Towns Act of 1946.

Now of course physical planning is not in itself a solution to problems of poverty and inequality (it is a dangerous illusion to attribute such a function to the planning system, the education system, or to social welfare provision) but the plight of London, Liverpool, Glasgow and the other great cities, far from demonstrating that dispersal was a misguided policy, shows that only one half of the formula has been put into effect. Behind the New Town policy, behind the various attempts to pursue a coherent policy on industrial location, has been a corollary which has not been followed. From Ebenezer Howard to those planners who invented unattractive words like "decanting" and "overspill" the ideology has had a two-fold implication. Not only would the planned transfer of families and jobs provide a better and more ample life for the working-class families who moved out, just as it did for the middle-class families who voted with their feet or their tyres for living out of town, but it would also improve conditions for those who remained behind, enabling the inner city to be redeveloped or rehabilitated at lower densities with a generous provision of open space. But Howard had another vision which he called "the social city". He thought that the future lay with the dispersed, poly-nuclear or many-centred city or city region, fulfilling the age-old dream of combining the advantages of urban and rural life. Kropotkin, Thomas More, and the authors of the *Blueprint for Survival*[3] shared the same conviction, and today Murray Bookchin remarks that the call for decentralised communities based on an ecological outlook is not going to die out again because of "the harsh fact that few choices are left today for the existing society."

34

References

[1] Murray Bookchin: *The Limits of City* (Black Rose, rev. ed. 1996).
[2] Ebenezer Howard: *Garden Cities of Tomorrow* (first published 1898, various editions available).
[3] *A Blueprint for Survival* (Penguin Special, rev. ed. 1973).

The Shires of Southern Britain

Dartington Hall Seminar, 4-6 November 1994

Participants will remember the engineer L.C.T. Rolt, a campaigner for the revival of inland waterways and for saving the integrity of the railway network that the Victorian engineers left behind. He was regarded as an awkward idiosyncratic character, but a few years ago his book *High Horse Riderless* was rediscovered by the eco-lobby and reissued by Green Books of Devon.[1]

And in 1992 Alan Sutton Publishers brought out Rolt's third volume of autobiography, *Landscape with Figures,*[2] written shortly before his death twenty years ago. In the course of it he describes changes in the West Country village where his family lived:

> Because of mis-application of the well-intentioned Slum Clearance Act by a zealous Medical Officer of Health, most of the old village cottages I knew were condemned on grounds of their low ceilings, or lack of through ventilation. Even with the aid of the available local authority grants, their occupants could not afford alterations which would conform with local regulations. Consequently, such houses have been acquired by those who could afford reconstruction, executives or retired business men, with the result that they have been 'prettified' beyond recognition and embellished with such things as bogus wrought iron work of welded steel strip, carriage lanterns or wooden wheelbarrows filled with flowers. Meanwhile such old village families as have survived this upheaval live in council houses on the village outskirts from whence they are collected and delivered daily by special coaches which take them to work in the nearby factories.

Here is the authentic voice of the pugnacious Mr Rolt. But it brings to mind several forgotten bits of recent history. The first is that those pathetic and neglected cottages were knocked down by the thousand in the postwar decades as unfit for human habitation, before they were seen as precious relics of vernacular building. The second is that their inhabitants were thankful to be allocated one of the raw new council houses, with all those modest facilities that had been beyond their reach for years.

The span of time between the writing and the publication of his book is a reminder of two other social facts. One is that those nearby factories were probably driven out of business in the early 80s. How thankful we'd all be today if they were still providing local employment. The other is that those council houses aren't being built any more, and all attempts to provide "affordable housing" for rent in the current political regime have to negotiate an impenetrable thicket of provisions to prevent them from moving up-market in the future, quite apart from the soaring price of land, and the shift in attitudes that makes all new building (apart from agricultural structures, thanks to the political influence of the farming industry) a blot on the landscape. The most vehement landscape cherishers are the new occupants of those picturesque cottages.

In my nearest village two parish councillors had laboured for years to bring a housing association proposal for affordable housing into existence. But the *East Anglian Daily Times* reports that by 25 votes to 15 a public meeting recommended that there was no need for new housing. Bryn Hurren, the parish vice-chairman, said that local people had been "mugged" by newcomers who had railroaded the meeting and forced a decision which went completely against previous, carefully researched opinion. Another councillor, Andrew Hazells said that the decision was "a nail in the coffin" of the younger generation. "I was born and bred here and think the people blocking this scheme should hang their heads in shame. The haves have delivered a very raw deal to the have-nots."

Of course the district council's planning committee may take a different view, but if it does, it will be accused of ignoring local opinion. What always surprises me is the blatancy with which the privileged present their case. They are not being selfish, they are protecting our common environment. John Brinckerhoff Jackson, the author of *Discovering the Vernacular Landscape*[3] remarks in a new book, "I am one of those who believe that our current guilt-ridden worship of the environment is a sign of moral and cultural disarray." My trouble is that I don't find much guilt in evidence.

However, the announcement of a conference on 27 September on "The Future of the Southern Shires" (organised by the Association of Small Historic Towns and Villages of the United Kingdom) includes a pungent quotation: "The Shires of Southern Britain are to the late twentieth century what the industrial towns of the north were to the beginning of the nineteenth, except that instead of attracting the rural poor they are attracting the urban rich."

We could pursue this analogy further and accept that the Victorian cities which expanded like mushrooms were an historical aberration brought about by the speed of industrialisation and that, just as Ebenezer Howard predicted, the twentieth century was bound to be "the period of the great exodus." The exodus of the footloose affluent who can buy their way in anywhere, doesn't help the urban poor with the same aspiration to join the trend, but it does destroy the hopes of low income rural families of getting a home in their own parish. In July, one of the CPRE's responses to the DOE publication *Quality in Town and Country* was to urge new approaches "to stem the out-migration of people and jobs from the towns and cities to the countryside." What measures will deter the urban rich from worsening the lives of the rural poor?

Their arrival doesn't improve the viability of local services. They don't use local shops, they rove in their Range Rovers. They don't improve the numbers at the village school, as their children are privately educated. They can afford to laugh at the county council's efforts to keep the buses on the road. They are certainly active in the village preservation society, since as the late Gerald Wibberley explained years ago, they "want their particular village to stay as it was when they decided to move there."

As to the measures needed to deter the urban poor from moving out of the city, they have existed for years. Maurice Ash, when chairman of the Town and Country Planning Association, declared that the combination of efforts to shore up the inner cities amounted, in practice, to nothing less than a conspiracy to *contain* the disadvantaged, "a conspiracy", he said, "because it suits the policies of our centralised state to keep the cities as prisons for the poor. It suits both those who want to manipulate the poor for reasons of power, and those who want to keep them from the preserves of the rich."

To my mind, the conspiracy to exclude the poor from rural England is the first item on the agenda in any discussion of the future of the shires.

Another familiar name for participants is that of Flora Thompson, the village postmistress's assistant of a century ago, who on the eve of the second world war began her trilogy of recollections of rural life, *Lark Rise to Candleford*. Many years earlier, in February 1925, just when the Elmhirsts were beginning their experiment in rural reconstruction, she noted down the characteristics of farm hedges:

> The hedgerow is so crammed with interest that it would provide studies for more hours than there are in the day. It is one of the old double hedges which, thickened with trees and twined about with creepers, used to be a common feature in English scenery. Such hedgerows used to be, and still are, where they have been retained, both gardens for

every kind of wild flower and sanctuaries for birds and lesser animals... Such hedgerows are gradually disappearing, together with the small, irregularly shaped fields they bounded. The modern scientific farmer does not approve of such waste of space and harbourage for 'vermin'. In highly farmed districts, the old, untidy, picturesque hedgerow is doomed.

An especially interesting thing about this passage is its date. For she was writing during the inter-war depression, long before what we now see as the agricultural industry's assault on trees and hedges began. At the Town and Country Planning Summer School at Lancaster in 1993, Sir Richard Body claimed that "The intensification of agriculture in the last 25 years has gone ahead faster and more furiously in the United Kingdom than in any other member state of the EC," and he read out to the assembled planners what he called "the woeful litany of statistics" of damage to the rural environment. These included:

130,000 miles of hedgerows ripped up.
40 per cent of our ancient woodlands gone.
7 million acres of pastureland ploughed up.
Over 95 per cent of our wetlands drained.
875 miles of stone wall destroyed.
95 per cent of the downlands of southern England gone.
180,000 acres of moorland ploughed up.

"Some of us," he said, "have made such an uproar about this agri-vandalism that in recent years we have seen the introduction of several schemes to undo the damage." It infuriates people like him (and me) that having paid subsidies for years to farmers to do all this damage in the name of increased output, we are now "paying the farmer to manage the countryside and thus protect the rural environment."

I remember the same bemusement not far from where I live, where farmers had received grants from the Ministry of Agriculture to grub up hedges, and I now saw a swarm of young people, employed under one of the bewildering set of acronyms, YTS, MSC, etc., replacing them at the public expense. I consoled myself with the thought that at least they were getting a training which will be important in the eco-conscious 21st century. For planting, nurturing and maintaining trees is a skill that has to be learned.

Where I live, for example, the nearby Dedham Vale is designated as an AONB (Area of Outstanding Natural Beauty) where the local planning authority has been given powers to preserve and enhance the area and to obtain Exchequer grants for this purpose. I watched with pleasure the enthusiasm of the people in charge, seeking to pass on wisdom and employability to the young whose job prospects around here are virtually non-existent. Elsewhere in the county, the National Trust in another AONB employs contractors, who employ subcontractors, to carry out the same planting function.

One young man from the next village (I'll call him Geoff) has at last found the right field of work for him as a result of the six years of experience he has gathered this way in tree planting and maintenance. In the off-season he finds work in associated jobs like fencing. Like anyone else, he has the urge to find a place of his own and conceived the idea that the thing to do was to find a patch of land for a tree nursery, so that he could win work supplying, planting and maintaining trees.

Land round here is absurdly expensive (thanks to subsidised farming) but some way north of here he has found a five-acre site, and has accumulated over those six years enough in the way of savings for a deposit on that site. You will have guessed that Geoff's plan would be to plant the site and live there in a caravan, supporting himself working for forestry subcontractors and fencing until the income from his saplings would enable him to replace the caravan and build himself a house.

Naturally local anarchist advice in the pub was that it was a great idea and he should just press ahead and do it. He would make a nice martyr to the Do Your Own Thing

41

ideology. Fortunately he is wiser than that, and knew that, quite apart from incurring the retributive wrath of the planning system, he would need every kind of approval, simply for the difficult task of getting a loan for the balance of the purchase price.

So he went to the regional office of the Ministry of Agriculture and ADAS (Agricultural Development and Advisory Service). He found both helpful but discouraging. They advised him that any other use of those five acres would be considered more viable and that the stumbling block was that the key issue was whether 70 per cent of his income would come from that site. It wouldn't. The local planning authority seemed to Geoff less friendly. No more mobile homes would be allowed on their patch. If he cared to put in an outline planning application (and pay a fee of £150) he could be told this officially.

So Geoff is resigned that he can't pursue his plan, and is looking still further afield for some area where land is less precious to try again. What should I advise him? I think that, unlike so many of the young, he has found his metier (or as our rulers would call it, his market niche) which is more than can be said of many of his contemporaries, thanks to the collapse of the job market. His occupation is geared to environmental priorities for the next century. He doesn't want subsidising like the farming industry. He doesn't demand "affordable" housing. He simply wants to house himself at the level he can afford and to improve his situation over time, just as all our rural ancestors did.

Yet somehow the rural environment is too precious to make room for people like him, whose whole precarious livelihood has grown out of the effort to improve it.

What can we conclude from my homely case-studies? My own conclusion is that a combination of protective legislation and market forces ensures that anyone who can afford to do so can live in the southern lowlands of Britain. See the property advertisements every week in

Country Life or in any estate agent's window. But young people from low-income families, whether rural or urban, are denied any opportunity to build a future by their own efforts in the southern lowlands of Britain. They are excluded by the property market, and by legislation introduced to "protect" the countryside.

References

[1] L.C.T. Rolt: *High Horse Riderless* (Green Books, 1988).
[2] L.C.T. Rolt: *Landscape with Figures* (Alan Sutton, 1992).
[3] John Brinckerholt Jackson: *Discoving the Vernacular Landscape* (Yale UP, 3rd ed. 1984).

Who Owns Nature? Possession and Dispossession

'Second Nature' Seminar at the Institute of
Contemporary Arts, London, November 1984

At a time when land ownership is being concentrated into fewer hands, concern is growing about the destruction of our wildlife, landscape and the social structure of rural communities; the increasing homogeneity of the countryside and the severance of our links with the past. Modern agricultural practices are making us feel like trespassers in our own land.

Cherished corners of the landscape can be changed beyond recognition in a few hours. Trees, streams, footpaths, buildings, symbols of permanence which transcend ownership, may suddenly disappear.

Who should decide the future of our countryside and wildlife? Should landless voyeurs be entitled to more than a view? Should everyone own a piece of land? What privileges and obligations does land ownership bring? Is the cult of reverence for special places and rare plants and animals robbing us of our common cultural inheritance? Whose countryside is it? Should we have more rights to walk the land?

***

Like just about every culture in the world, from the American Indians to the Patagonians or the Australian aborigines, we have a great creative legend on the underside of our history that the land belongs to the people and that every family has its right to the livelihood they can gain from their portion of it. How absurd that any of us should have been so deluded by acceptance of the status quo as to imagine that any other version of natural law could be true.

The last speaker, Fraser Harrison, has a passage in his book *Strange Land,*[1] describing the effect of the enclosures on poor rural dwellers. "Clinging to the bottom of rural society" he says, "was a multifarious population of smallholders, cottagers and landless workers, who gained a precarious livelihood by dint of dividing their family energy between domestic industry, occasional or regular work for wages and subsistence cultivation yielding a small, unreliable extra for the market. These people and their animals depended on the usage of common land, which was usually sanctioned by custom, but seldom by law. With the enclosure, or in some instances, unashamed confiscation of common land, followed by the automatic cancellation of customary rights and privileges, the cottager and the squatter were summarily stripped of their ramshackle independence and reduced to living entirely off the sale of their labour power."

Now for well over a hundred years, the descendants of some of those people, driven into towns and cities as wage-slaves of the industrial revolution, have yearned to recover something of that rural heritage. They *want* that ramshackle independence. They *want* to live in the country and pick up a living whatever way they can. This is often mistaken for, or patronised as, ordinary urban sentimentality about the country, but I am convinced that it is something different.

The aristocracy have always taken it for granted that the country is the only place to live, with a town house for the winter. The upper middle-classes have always taken it for granted that people like themselves lived in both town and country, the middle middle-classes live in the country and commute to town, or live in the town and have a country cottage. The lower middle-classes live in suburbs, and, with that insufferable English snobbery we all have to live with, are despised just for doing so by people who take for granted that wider choice that money can so easily give. Though, if they are nature-lovers, they will have learned from Richard Mabey that every suburb is one big nature reserve, providing a bosky habitat for all those species for whom the countryside is nowadays less welcoming because of the activities of the cereal-producing industry and its subcontractors.

Poor people, on the other hand, live in high-density urban ghettos, surrounded by dereliction, or in crumbling council estates on the fringe which have somehow not developed those characteristics of leafy suburbia. The economic expansion which caused our cities to grow like mushrooms in the nineteenth century, absorbing all those super-numerary yokels, has evaporated and has been doing so for many years. Outward movement from the overcrowded cities has been a characteristic of the entire twentieth century, and the ability to make this move has been absolutely taken for granted by everyone above a certain income level.

When poor people aspire to join the rural-dwelling section of society too, it is grotesquely patronising to assume that they, unlike us, have simply been led astray by the images conveyed by margerine adverts on the telly. Nor should we assume that they are among the people lampooned by John Barrell in his sharp little contribution to the book *Second Nature*.[2] They are not looking back to an imaginary Golden Age, they are not seeking some elusive self-sufficiency, and they are not subscribers to what he calls a generally-diffused and thoroughly nostalgic conservationist sentiment. They are looking for exactly the same things that anyone else who lives in the country by choice is seeking. They just have less access to cash or credit to do it with.

My own contribution to the book *Second Nature* is about the one example in our recent history when it was possible for poor urban dwellers to have a place in the country, and is in fact a brief summary of the findings of Dennis Hardy and me in yet another book, called *Arcadia for All; The Legacy of a Makeshift Landscape*.[3] It's about that period between the turn of the century and the outbreak of the second world war when, because of agricultural depression, land was dirt cheap. In marginal areas, where land went out of farming use first, speculators, who were the only purchasers at auctions, divided land into plots which were sold to the buyers, usually poor city dwellers, enticed down by free food and rail tickets, to build their dream home, shed, shack, shanty, converted railway carriage, holiday home or smallholding.

Plenty of them succeeded, and what started as the holiday home when the children were young became the permanent home, either after the bombing of the cities in the war or later as the retirement home of the original pioneer settlers. The small-holders, chicken rearers, or coypu- or mink-raisers, were usually unsuccessful, but they often clung on to their holdings, as there was nothing else to do, and made what they could of their ramshackle independence. In the course of time their children, or sons or daughters-in-law, were grateful inheritors, glad of a place of their own in the country.

We have spelt out this particular history and I need to remind you that far from being enemies of what we have chosen to call 'nature', the plotlanders, unlike the people who effortlessly inherited vast tracts of England, have proved to be nature's best friends. The plotlands, as Oliver Rackham remarks in his book on ancient woodlands, "are of value for wildlife because of their varied structure and freedom from agricultural pressures."

But of course it was the humble plotlanders who were hammered by the ruralist lobby. If you read the pre-war literature of planning and conservation you are made aware of the intense horror that was felt by all right-thinking (that is, privileged) people at the desecration of the landscape they thought they saw happening everywhere. Dean Inge, a celebrated publicist of the period, coined the phrase 'bungaloid growth' with its implication that some kind of cancer was spreading over the face of the Home Counties. Howard Marshall, in the compendium called *Britain and the Beast*,[4] published in 1937, declared that "a gimcrack civilisation crawls like a giant slug over the country, leaving a foul trail of slime behind it."

We can't help feeling in retrospect that part of this disgust at the incursion of ignorant town-dwellers into the countryside (which of course they couldn't appreciate, could they?) was ordinary snobbish misanthropy. The wrong sort of people were getting a place in the sun.

There was all-party support for the legislation we have nowadays to protect the country from the incursion of ordinary town-dwellers, while preserving it for the activities of the agricultural industry. You can draw your own conclusions about who owns nature.

I myself have no doubt about what cause to support, and it is that minute political lobby that wants poor people to be able to move to the country. This could be the Greentown Group from Milton Keynes or it could be the promotion by the Town and Country Planning Association of the Lightmoor Project at Telford New Town in Shropshire. There are vast numbers of people who want nothing more than that ramshackle independence they think they can gain from living in the country. There exists, for example, a book called the *Rural Resettlement Handbook*,[5] packed with useful advice for people with this aspiration to move out of town. It came from a publisher no-one had ever heard of, it never got advertised, but in the late 70s it went into two editions. Some people were very anxious to learn what it could teach them. It has now been completely rewritten and has come out again in a new third edition, and I, without any axe to grind, want to recommend it to anybody here with that urge to move to the country.

The continued demand for that particular book, with its ordinary prosaic advice, is one of several indications for me of the enormous groundswell of popular yearnings to live in the country. I respect these aspirations and I think it a fable for our time that the agricultural lobby

48

has ensured that it is exempt from the planning legislation that effectively prevents poor people from repopulating the country.

References

[1] Fraser Harrison: *Strange Land* (Sidgwick & Jackson, 1982).

[2] Richard Mabey, *et al.* (eds) *Second Nature* (Cape, 1984).

[3] Dennis Hardy and Colin Ward: *Arcadia For All* (Mansell, 1984; Five Leaves, 2003).

[4] Clough Williams-Ellis: *Britain and the Beast* (Dent, 1937).

[5] Dick Kitto: *Rural Resettlement Handbook* (Prism, 1984).

The Allotment Garden as a Green Affirmation

International Conference on Utopian Thought and
Communal Experience, at New Lanark, Scotland,
20 July 1988

You will be astonished that in the context of dreams of
utopia and communalistic experiments, my subject is a
feature of life as ordinary and prosaic as that of allotment
gardening, and since this is an international gathering, I
should say that in the United States they are called
(because of wartime experience) Liberty Gardens or
Victory Gardens, but more recently, community gardens.
In Italy they are *orti urbani,* in Germany they are called
Schrebergärten or *Kleingärten,* in the Netherlands,
Volkstuinen, in France, *Jardins Familiaux,* in Spain
Huertos Comunales.

Their importance in the present context is that since in
Britain, local authorities have a legal responsibility to
provide them on demand, they are the only embodiment
in the law of a universal myth: that of the natural right
of human beings to the use of land.

When we call this a myth we are not implying that it is
a fiction. Quite the contrary, it is an obvious truth. We
mean that all through history in most of the cultures that
we know about, people have claimed that there was a
time in the past when the land was held in common, and
that all through the history of popular and political
uprisings, people have evoked this communal past as a
symbol of the rights for whose restoration they were
struggling, and that all through the history of utopian
writings and aspirations, the right of access to land for
food production has been a key issue. In our parochial
British political history, the slogan "three acres and a

cow" a century ago struck a nerve of popular utopianism which has by no means died away today.[1] When Peter Kropotkin made a world survey, historically and geographically, of mutual aid as a more important factor in evolution than mutual competition, he found that:

> As to private property in land, the village community did not, and could not, recognise anything of the kind, and, as a rule, it does not recognise it now. The land was the common property of the tribe... and the village community itself owned its part of the tribal territory so long only as the tribe did not claim a redistribution of the village allotments. The clearing of woods and the breaking of the prairies being mostly done by the communities or, at least, by the joint work of several families — always with the consent of the community — the cleared plots were held by each family for a term of four, twelve, or twenty years, after which term they were treated as parts of the arable land owned in common. Private property, or possession 'for ever', was as incompatible with the very principles and the religious conceptions of the village community as it was with the principle of the *gens*; so that a long influence of the Roman law and the Christian Church, which soon adopted the Roman principles, were required to accustom the barbarians to the idea of private property in land being possible.[2]

This theme reverberates throughout utopian writings,[3] and in English history is enshrined in the story of Gerard Winstanley and the Diggers, assertion of the right to dig, a story more celebrated today than it was in 1649 when Britain was not a United Kingdom, but was a Commonwealth or republic. The Diggers' invasion of 'common land' next to Campe Close at St George's Hill, at Walton-on-Thames in Surrey, began on the first of April that year, and the Council of State was immediately informed by a local landowner that people were sowing the ground with parsnips, carrots and beans, with the intention of restoring "the ancient community of enjoying the fruits of the earth." The Council of State sent the letter on to Lord Fairfax, Lord General of the Armed Forces of the Commonwealth, urging him to send some forces "to Cobham in Surrey and thereabouts, with orders to disperse the people so met, and to prevent the like for the future, that a malignant and disaffected party may not under colour of such a ridiculous people have any opportunity to rendezvous themselves in order to do a greater mischief."[4]

They were driven out, their vegetables uprooted and their huts burned. Within eighteen months at least nine other Digger colonies were set up and evicted. The events of 1649 were a dramatisation of a process which had and has been a continuous feature of British history: the enclosure of the land by the rich and powerful, and the encroachment on the land by the poor and hungry. Tradition and a sense of natural justice, as well as the imperative need to feed a family which is felt by insects, mammals and birds as well as by humans, gave the inhabitants of any place the right to the products of woods, forests, rivers and stream, the right to pasture domesticated animals and to hunt, trap or fish wild creatures, as well as to till the soil in what became known as the common fields. These rights were safeguarded by elaborate local rules and conventions, designed from experience to prevent exploitation of the self-balancing subsistence economy by those who chose to demand too much and consequently to deny the rights of others.

For the ancient ideal of communal access to land has two separate components. One is that of collective cultivation and the other is that co-operating individuals or families each have a right to their own patch. The modern history of the Soviet Union and its satellite nations in East Europe, or of China, exhibit the recent evolution of both these ideals. Long before, and certainly since, the collapse of the Soviet empire, every family that could manage it, struggled for a patch of ground to ensure its vegetables. In Britain, even John Locke, who believed that the sole end of government was the preservation of property, declared that "As much land as a man tills, plants, improves, cultivates and comes into the product of, so much is his property."[5]

In the folklore, not only of Britain but of many other parts of Europe, and consequently in the New World, there were innumerable variations on this formula. (As much as he could enclose in the night within the throw of an axe from the dwelling, was the formula in Radnorshire in Wales). In rural England a vast number of commoners, cottagers or squatters lived from their tiny parcels of land and/or their rights in the common fields, common grazing, woods and "wastes". Winstanley, like many others, held the view that the Norman Conquest of 1066 had deprived the people of their land and that with the defeat of Charles I, as ultimate heir of William I, the people had won back their right to the land, by right of conquest.

Over many centuries, landlords sequestered land from this common stock in a continuous process culminating in the period of Parliamentary Enclosures between the years 1750 and 1850. This final campaign of enclosing the common land gave birth to the modern allotment movement.

The land that was belatedly "allotted" to the poor was an inadequate recompense, historically speaking a derisory compensation, for a customary communality in access to land that was more than a myth: it had been continuous from our remotest ancestors. Thus the authoritative historians of the remaining common lands in England and Wales, W.G. Hoskins and Dudley Stamp, concluded that "Common rights were not something specifically granted by a generous landlord, but were the residue of rights that were once more extensive, rights that in all probability antedate the idea of private property in land, and are therefore of vast antiquity."[6]

With the sanction of the state, and with only a handful of exceptions, the last vestiges of these common rights were extinguished. Just because of its significance in

British history, the enclosure of fields and wastes is one of the most fiercely debated aspects of this history among professional historians. One generation of historians (Slater, Hasbach and J.L. & Barbara Hammond[7]) presented a picture of the devastation of the lives of most rural dwellers caused by the Enclosures. A later school, now known as the revisionists, contradicted this interpretation, using words like 'mistaken', 'exaggerated', 'overdrawn', 'unrealistic', 'unhistorical', 'partial' and 'tendentious', 'seriously astray', 'biased', and 'illiberal'.[9]

Needless to say, a still more recent group of scholars, the counter-revisionists, have provided a mountain of evidence to support the earlier point of view,[10] and the recent historical re-appraisal of open field agriculture has established that "the open fields were far more open to innovation and flexible agriculture than once supposed" and that "the account of them as seriously backward and by nature inhibitive of new techniques is most certainly incorrect."[11]

Slowly and patchily in the 19th century, the provision of allotments for the poor became a condition in the succession of Enclosure Acts passed by Parliament. Their advocacy was often from outside the ranks of the poor, who, it was thought, could find in allotment gardens a means by which they could, through diligence and self-help, both feed their families and add to the family income. This is why John Stuart Mill claimed that allotments were "a contrivance to compensate the labourer for the insufficiency of his wages by giving him something else as a supplement to them" and that in fact they were "a method of making people grow their own poor rate."[12]

The provision of allotments tended to be opposed by farmers and supported by the clergy, and slowly, through a historical sleight-of-hand, it became thought of as an act of charity rather than as a substitute for ancient rights. Within the modern allotment movement there are many who see it instead as yet another monument to those expressions of working class self-help and mutual aid, like the friendly societies, the trade unions and the co-operative movement, which were a working class response to the devastating impact of the industrial revolution in nineteenth century Britain. Thus a modern plot-holder writes:

> Too many people have a wrong impression about allotments. The movement is not wholly dependent for its well-being upon the encouragement given to it by government and local authorities... Allotments had their origin in self-help (not charity) and even now the concept of self-help remains fundamental... Throughout its entire history the motive force behind the allotment movement has always been self-help. This is exemplified by the labourers displaced from the countryside during the periodic down-turns in the trade cycle that punctuated Victorian times, who, being forced to seek work in the towns (often working 55 hours a week in the dreariest of employments), eagerly canvassed alternatives to factory work, and were only too keen to turn to spade husbandry whenever the opportunity arose... It is surprising that so many found the strength and determination and genuine love of gardening needed to tend their allotments, yet here are signs of a deep working-class sentiment and attitude.[13]

Thanks to continued political agitation in the nineteenth century, the allotment movement is by now as much an urban and suburban as a rural phenomenon. Local authorities (district and parish councils) have a statutory duty to provide allotments for their resident citizens, provided for by Section 23 of the Small Holdings and Allotments Act of 1908. But of course the law does not say where, when or how soon the citizens can have their plots. Some have waiting lists, others have embarrassingly empty ground. The law of allotments is immensely complex and contradictory and long in need of simplification. There is no very clear definition of what an allotment is, but Section 22 of the Allotments Act of 1922 says that an allotment garden is "an allotment not exceeding forty poles in extent which is wholly or mainly cultivated by the occupier for the production of vegetables or fruit crops for consumption by himself or his family." A pole is a little over 30 square yards. The standard size of an allotment plot is 10 rods or 300 square yards (250 square metres).

But by now you will be wondering whether this particular token survival of the ancient communality of land has any significance in contemporary Britain. One answer is that gardening is the most popular active leisure pursuit in this country just as it is in America and in many other lands. Even though a far greater proportion of households have a garden attached to the house than did in the earlier decades of this century, there are today about half a million allotments in Britain. Numbers have fluctuated enormously because of the impact of the two wars, as in every other belligerent country, on allotment holding. The figure rose from about 580,000 in 1914 to 1,330,000 in 1920, and from about 815,000 in England and Wales in 1939 to perhaps 1,600,000 in 1945. A sharp post-war decline led the government in 1965 to invite the late Harry Thorpe, professor of geography at Birmingham University, to chair a Departmental Committee of Inquiry "to review general policy on allotments in the light of present-day conditions in England and Wales, and to recommend what legislative and other changes, if any, are needed." This committee reported in 1969 with dozens of recommendations, none of which has been acted upon by any subsequent government.[14] Thorpe saw the allotment movement as a dwindling bunch of old men, its image tainted by an atmosphere of poverty and charity. He wanted a consolidation of allotment law into one Act, a recognition that allotment gardening was part of the "leisure" provision by local authorities, who did not stint on investment in other forms of leisure, and a commitment to "changing the image" as well as the atmosphere of the allotment site from utilitarian vegetable patches to the Leisure Garden which was a facility for the whole family, with its flowers, lawns and chalets, suitably serviced and maintained. Thorpe's committee had been deeply influenced by the evolution of leisure gardens in several European countries.

Although the government took no action, several local authorities, notably Birmingham, began to upgrade their allotment sites to leisure gardens, and the National Society to which local allotment societies were affiliated voted to change its name to the National Society of Leisure Gardeners. Several years later, as a result of a trend known as the Yorkshire Backlash, it reinstated the hallowed word "allotment" in its title.[15] And there were others who felt that this last survival of ancient communal rights was something distinct from a mere hobby. Irene Evans, who has studied the allotment movement here in Scotland, wrote that, even though many recreations fulfil deep-seated personal and social needs, "the right to grow some of your own food is fundamentally different from any right you might have to score a goal or sink a putt."[16]

Thorpe's forbodings of inevitable decline did not come true. For in the 1970s the new environmental conscious-ness, ideas of self-sufficiency, and the upsurge of enthusiasm for fresh and organically-grown food, brought a new influx of demand for allotments. A report from Friends of the Earth in 1979 claimed that "Nearly all towns and cities in Great Britain are experiencing a boom in the interest shown in allotments. In England and Wales, the waiting list for allotments has gone up a staggering 1,600 per cent."[17]

The demand for allotments has stabilised in the 1980s. As with the distribution of affordable housing, there are empty plots in some areas and an unfulfilled demand in others. My impression is that both local societies and their national organisation are ill-equipped to withstand the pressures on local authorities to dispose of land for more profitable uses, though there have been some notable victories when allotment-holders have fought for their statutory rights.

But what remains of that ancient communality when the image of the allotment-holder is of an isolated individualist, caring for little beyond his or her plot and shed? Below the organisational level, we have observed an intense expression of mutual aid among allotment gardeners, and one which transcends the racial divisions of British society in other fields. It could reflect the common pursuit of gardening and the consequent sharing of wisdom, experience, seeds and produce. Or it could be a reminder of the ancient shared ideal of communal access to land, expressed by Robert Frost in his lines:

Men work together, I told him from the heart
Whether they work together or apart.

References

[1] *The Radical Programme* (Chapman and Hall 1885) proposed that "Besides the creation of smallholdings, local authorities should have compulsory powers to purchase land where necessary at a fair market-price... for the purpose of garden and field allotments, to be let at fair rents to all labourers who might desire them, in plots up to one acre of arable and three or four acres of pasture."

[2] Peter Kropotkin: *Mutual Aid; A Factor of Evolution* (William Heinemann, 1902, new edition Freedom Press, 1987).

[3] Marie Louise Berneri: *Journey Through Utopia* (Routledge and Kegan Paul, 1951, new edition Freedom Press, 1980).

[4] Lewis H. Berens: *The Digger Movement in the Days of the Commonwealth* (1906, new edition Holland Press and Merlin Press, 1961).

[5] John Locke: *An Essay Concerning the True Original Extent and End of Civil Government* Chapter VI, para 31. (1690, Penguin Classics, 1970).

[6] W.G. Hoskins and L. Dudley Stamp: *The Common Lands of England and Wales* (Collins, 1963).

[7] G. Slater: *The English Peasantry and the Enclosure of the Common Fields* (1907); W. Hasbach; *A History of the English Agricultural Labourer* (1908): J.L. & Barbara Hammond: *The*

Village Labourer (1911).

[8] J.D. Chambers "Enclosure and Labour Supply in the Industrial Revolution" in D.V. Glass and D.E.C. Eversley (eds) *Population in History* (Edward Arnold, 1965); J.D. Chambers and G.E. Mingay: *The Agricultural Revolution 1750-1880* (Batsford, 1966) and J.A. Yelling: *Common Field and Enclosure in England 1450-1850* (Macmillan, 1977).

[9] List of adjectives gathered by K.D.M. Snell from the writings of G.E. Mingay.

[10] Michael Turner: *Enclosures in Britain 1750-1830* (Macmillan, 1984).

[11] K.D.M. Snell: *Annals of the Labouring Poor: Social Change and Agrarian England 1660-1900 (Cambridge University Press, 1905).*

[12] J.S. Mill: *Principles of Political Economy,* Vol II (London, 1848).

[13] "The Allotments Movement" *The Recreational Gardener* (Journal of the London Association of Recreational Gardeners) No 14, Dec 1977.

[14] *Report of the Departmental Committee of Inquiry into Allotments* Cmnd 4166 (HMSO, 1969).

[15] National Society of Allotment and Leisure Gardeners Ltd, Hunters Road, Corby, Northants NN17 1JE.

[16] Irene Evans, letter to *New Statesman* 27 September 1985. See Irene Evans: "Allotment provision in Scotland 1985" in Irene Evans and Joy Hendry (eds) *The Land for the People* (Scottish Socialist Society, 1985).

[17] Peter Riley: *Economic Growth: The Allotments Campaign Guide* (Friends of the Earth, 1979).

A Century of Land-Settlement in Essex

Colchester Archaeological Group Winter Meetings
4 December 1989, Colchester Castle

Ladies and gentlemen, thank you for coming. I'm delighted to say that I have brought you here under false pretences. Let me explain why. For a long time now I have been a professional writer, and the books I work on tend to be about people's use of their environment. Now books don't bring in much money, but they do bring their writers a certain rather spurious prestige. So they get invited to address meetings. And the meetings bring you in touch with people's precious and unique nuggets of information and experience on some aspect of a subject.

The tragedy is that by then it is too late. The book is out. And if it is the kind of book I write, it is very unlikely to reach a second, revised edition. Worse than that, whether it is a good or bad book, its existence has ensured that no publisher is going to invest in another book on the same rather specialist topic for a good many years.

David Crouch of Kelvedon, and I, wrote a book about the culture of the allotment. And whenever we talked about it people at the meeting came out with marvellous observations from their own experience which we could not exploit. Dennis Hardy from Brentwood, and I, wrote a book about the history of holiday camps, and when we talked about it, people told us of their experiences, working for Butlin in Clacton or Warner at Dovercourt in the late 1930s. We also wrote a book about the 'plotlands' or unofficial settlements that people built for themselves in the inter-war period. It led me to an invitation to talk here, to the Colchester Archaeological Group, about the history of Jaywick Sands, and needless to say, people kindly came along with all sorts of contributions to that history, too late for us to make use of it.

You notice that I used the word 'exploit', because that in fact is what historians, at least of my kind, do. There was a wise remark by the architectural philosopher W.R. Lethaby. He said that "History is written by those who survive. Those who went under had the experience."

I am sure that this is true of the experience of land settlement, and the reason why I admit to bringing you here under false pretences is is that I know hardly anything about a century of land settlement in Essex. Somebody here is bound to know more and it is sensible for me to make contact with such people before, rather than after, I have attempted to write a book on the subject.

By Land Settlement, I mean policies, governmental, semi-official or unofficial, of settling people on the land in order to enable them to earn a living by farming or horticulture. Such policies have been adopted in many countries. They were used in the development of the American West, and much later as part of Roosevelt's New Deal. They were used by the British in encouraging emigration to its colonies, by Mussolini in populating reclaimed land in the Pontine marshes and in promoting white settlement in Italy's colonial empire. Both dictatorial and democratic governments have used strategies of this kind.

They have encouraged it too on a domestic scale, here at home. The century I refer to is the hundred years between the Allotments Extension Act of 1882, consolidated by the Small Holdings and Allotments Act of 1908, and the closure by the Ministry of Agriculture of the Land Settlement Association in 1982.

There were a variety of motives for supporting resettlement on the land. They began with attempts to stem the 'drift from the land' during the late Victorian period of agricultural depression and mechanisation when any urban occupation earned far higher wages, and

61

continued with one effort after another to provide displaced farm labourers, reformed inebriates, paupers, soldiers returning from the First World War, and the inter-war urban unemployed with a livelihood on smallholdings.

In the post-1915 years, such holdings, originally provided by philanthropists, then by county councils under mandatory legislation, and then by central government itself, have been seen as 'the first rung on the farming ladder' for would-be farmers who, with the inflation of land prices and rents, could never hope to set up on their own in any other way.

Few of these ventures can be said to have succeeded, even though some managed to overcome the inherent problems of small-scale producers (the fact, for example that they are obliged to buy at retail prices and sell at wholesale prices). The Land Settlement Association organised large-scale marketing, linked with the major retail outlets. Today, for example, Norfolk County Council has a long waiting list for holdings, but an insistent demand from existing tenants for the amalgamation of sites into what are perceived as viable units.

The remarkable thing is that there remains an incredibly widespread dream of settling on a small patch of land to gain a livelihood, and in fact the queue of would-be smallholders is lengthening, while current Europe-wide over-production of agricultural crops brings a demand for the subdivision of large farms as land is set aside from cereal production. There is also a rapidly growing interest in organic cultivation. The actual experience of land settlement is thus a matter of great current interest.

But I am concerned with the impact of land settlement on Essex. The county has of course always had a special relationship with London. Roman London was fed from the fields of the Tower Hamlets. By the seventh century London re-emerged as the capital of Essex and for centuries the Essex side of the city was full of market gardens, moving steadily eastwards through the nineteenth century, Stratford, West Ham, Barking, Rainham, Dagenham, Hornchurch and Somford with further pockets at Stifford, Horndon, Tilbury, Avely, Thurrock and Stanford-le-Hope.

The Thames was the basis of a beautifully-balanced transport economy of spritsail barges using the river ports of Essex, Kent and Suffolk. The barges which carried the bricks that built nineteenth century London returned loaded with refuse from the city's rubbish dumps, which not only fired the kilns of the Kent and Essex brickyards but also raised the level of the marshlands. The barges which carried straw, food and fodder to a city dependent on horses would return with dung and stable litter for the farms and market gardens. Innumerable daily transactions as well as a vast river traffic linked the riverside parishes of London with Essex.

So when the cry of *Back to the Land* arose in the city, it was natural that Essex should be the first port of call. George Lansbury, for example, a celebrated and much-loved East London politician, had a continual interest in the efforts of Londoners to make a more ample life for themselves in the abandoned farmlands of South Essex, and, when leader of the Labour Party in 1934, declared that "I just long to see a start made on this job of reclaiming, recreating rural England."

There is a book by an American scholar, Martin Wiener, called *English Culture and the Decline of the Industrial Spirit 1850-1980,*[1] which has been, in a rather third-hand way, very influential among the intellectual mentors of our present government. Regardless of this particular influence, Wiener has some interesting comments to make on "schemes for the creation of smallholdings, despite the lack of grass-roots demand in England (such as certainly existed in Ireland) for such land distribution." He cites various pieces of research to indicate that the "economic case for smallholdings was weak, and that the policy was advocated and supported for social rather than economic reasons." He quotes the view of the sociologist O.R. McGregor: "The pathetic delusion that some sort of land settlement scheme contained the secret cure for the ills of industrial society had great survival value" and concludes that "the land reform issue drew its greatest support from the new professional classes, for whom it was less an economic issue than a moral (and cultural, we might add) one." He adds that "In England the issue remained in the realm of symbol and myth."

Well, of course, it didn't. Real people with real hopes and aspirations were involved in the schemes that others dreamed up for them in land settlement. Essex was the nearest available place for all their aspirations. For apart from the ancient river routes there were two rival railway lines serving the area. And land was incredibly cheap. The agricultural depression that began in the 1870s and continued with a few hiccups like the First World War, until the Second World War, hit Essex severely. There were endless forced sales and quite often no buyers. The exceptions were Scottish immigrants, frustrated in their attempts to get land at home, who moved south and were very often successful, and speculators like Frederick Francis Ramuz, Mayor of Southend, who bought vast areas of south Essex when there were no other purchasers. There is an invisible geological line across Essex, running through places like the village of Stock, below which the soil with its heavy clay is what farmers used to call "three-horse land". The bankruptcies happened there first, and as few people wanted to buy the land as farms, it was divided up into small plots where Londoners could put up their weekend retreats, holiday homes, chicken farms or, as a last hope, smallholdings. The story is told in the book by Dennis Hardy and me called *Arcadia for All.*[2]

In another book of Dennis Hardy's, *Alternative Communities in Nineteenth Century England,*[3] he describes among many others, a whole series of communitarian land ventures in Essex from the end of that century. Quite apart from the demand of the Liberal politician Jesse Collings for "three acres and a cow", there were various charitable and propagandist organisations advocating the recolonisation of England by both the rural and the urban unemployed through land colonies and smallholdings. There was also the impact of that whole movement of revulsion against the horrors of Victorian industrial life and the hypocrisies of Victorian middle-class life, reflected in the urge to go "back to the land" reflected in the Tolstoyan, socialist and anarchist movements, and the cult of the "simple life".

In 1896 a group of disciples of Tolstoy, including his translator Aylmer Maude and his friend the Russian exile Vladimir Tchertkoff, bought ten acres of land at Cocks Clark near Purleigh. They raised vegetables, planted fruit trees, made in their first year about 7,000 bricks and built a hundred foot greenhouse, and acquired cows, goats and chickens, as well as a pony and cart to take their produce to market at Maldon, five miles away. Alas, by 1899 they were writing to Tolstoy to tell him of the collapse of their experiment.

In 1897 another group of Tolstoyan anarchists settled in the heart of the south Essex plotland belt, at The Chase, Ashingdon, near Hockley, led by James Evans, keeping goats and growing vegetables on his 4-acre plot. Long after the community itself had collapsed, its traces remained, as it was for many decades the home of the radical publisher C.W. Daniel. In 1898 another such group bought twenty-nine acres and three cottages for a total of £700 to the south of Downham Church and overlooking the Thames Valley at Wickford, cultivating small plots individually.

A far more serious venture in Essex was similarly inspired by a writer, Robert Blatchford. He had started the socialist journal *The Clarion* in 1891, and between 1892 and 1893 he serialised in it his *Merrie England* which, published as a book, sold nearly a million copies in the next few years. Blatchford called for a return to the land and included an idyllic description of a family living in rural bliss on three acres in Essex. This inspired a Manchester printer, Thomas Smith to change his occupation and move with his family in 1895 to eleven acres of heavy clay at Mayland near Althorne, and to advertise for fellow colonists. Dennis Hardy explains: "Although it was known locally as the 'new Jerusalem' the community achieved little success in its early days, either as an agricultural or as a socialist experiment. Smith himself was new to the land, and most of the early settlers came from urban occupations (clerks, schoolmasters, shop assistants, engineers and warehousemen). For a while Smith returned to Manchester to supplement his income, and from time to time took other jobs locally in Essex..." Another student of the 'Back to the Land' period observes that Smith, by contrast with many others among these hopeful colonists did not feel compromised by taking jobs to earn cash and was also capable of learning from his experience. He was, Jan Marsh explains, both pragmatic and resourceful:

> The most profitable produce at Mayland was tomatoes and other salad vegetables, and the earlier the crop the higher the price. Smith therefore steadily moved to cultivation under glass, producing strawberries, lettuce, tomatoes and even melons — all crops whose wholesale price was good even with small quantities. Gradually he acquired the knowledge and skill to make his holding into a thriving business. Later he published handbooks on intensive cultivation, although the picture they give of a scientifically-managed market garden with intensive manuring, acres of cold frames, carefully regulated cloches and a large packing shed is perhaps not the pastoral image Smith or others had before them when setting off back to the land.

Well, that is what Jan Marsh concludes, but Smith, as she says, was willing to learn from the experience he had gained, lessons acquired by many later smallholders. When Smith's book on what was known as "French Gardening" appeared in 1909 it had an introduction by Peter

Kropotkin, since it exemplified many of his contentions in his book *Fields, Factories and Workshops*,[4] a book which inspired generations of would-be small-holders.

But while stressing the very important influence of books in this whole movement, I must mention another. In 1890 General William Booth of the Salvation Army had published his book *In Darkest England and the Way Out*,[5] a devastating account of the condition of what he called the "submerged tenth" of the urban population. The way out suggested by him was responsible for a series of experiments in land settlement. At Hadleigh in Essex, between Benfleet and Southend, when land prices were at their lowest, the Salvation Army bought three thousand acres sloping down to the river. Down on the rough grazing near the river a brickworks and kilns were established, on an adjoining site was the settlement for inebriates. When the other Booth, Charles Booth the sociologist, visited the place, he reported that "On one hillside, beautifully placed, is the poultry farm with over 1,500 head of poultry, some of them prize birds... In other parts of the estate are the fruit gardens and orchards, the vegetable grounds... The industrial buildings include a well-appointed cowshed with accommodation for 100 head, piggeries and stores... There were in residence 250 colonists, and employment could be found for fifty more without further outlay." Ten years later Rider Haggard, reporting to the government in 1905 on rural resettlement schemes, was equally impressed. He commented, approvingly, on what he saw as the "kind but strict discipline" with which the colony was run, and explained that "A man is raised in his grade if he works well and satisfactorily and his general character and conduct are proved to be good. If he is raised to this higher class dormitory he is also raised to a higher class dietary and receives food of rather better quality and more ample in quantity."

To us, of course, it sounds like a prison sentence, and it seems to have been all-male and intended to prepare men for agricultural work overseas.

At the other end of Essex, at Boxted, near here, the Salvation Army promoted land settlement of 400 acres in 1906 as a result of a legacy from George Herring. The site was divided into eighty plots averaging five acres. The intention was to provide a house on each with initial capital for manures and seeds as well as tree-fruit and soft-fruit. A successful grower from the Vale of Evesham was one of the first settlers. Louisa Jebb reported in 1907 that "The distribution of the produce will be made an object of special attention. A society of the growers will be formed, and the produce will be collected, graded and distributed as a whole." The fact that I can, at the moment, tell you nothing about its evolution in the subsequent eighty years will tell you how much I have still to learn about this venture. I will find out.

Now I must return to the pragmatic and resourceful Thomas Smith. His rare qualities attracted the attention of an American philanthropist Joseph Fels, founder of the Fels-Naptha Soap Company. George Lansbury had drawn him to collaboration with the Boards of Poor Law Guardians in London under the provisions of the Unemployed Workmen's Act which granted government money to various local unemployment committees to enable them to find work. With his aid Lansbury set up "labour colonies" at Hollesley Bay in Suffolk and at Laindon in Essex, where the labour of 200 men, Lansbury claimed, "turned what was derelict land into orchards and gardens."

At Mayland, close to Thomas Smith's land, Fels bought the 600-acre Nipsells Farm with the aim of making it available in the form of smallholdings "as a long-term opportunity rather than for short-term relief." Dennis Hardy remarks that "Today the landscape of Mayland is still predominantly one of nurseries and smallholdings with a large number of glasshouses, the legacy of Smith and Fels. There have been few external changes to Smith's house, 'Homestead', and on the roadside can be bought fruit and vegetables from the formerly hostile soil."

But amongst this interesting assortment of idealistic, charitable, voluntary and philanthropic activity, what had happened to official support for land settlement?

The Small-holdings Act of 1892, the response to years of agitation, allowed county councils to buy or lease land, to provide fences, roads and buildings and subdivide it to resell on long-term cheap credit terms. Since would-be small-holders wanted to rent, rather than buy land, it was correctly described as a window-dressing act. By 1908 it had only provided 244 holdings. I don't know if any were in Essex.

The Local Government Act of 1894 empowered councils to provide for resale, both allotments and small-holdings. It provided very few smallholdings. It was the Small Holdings and Allotments Act of 1908 which at last enabled county councils to provide small-holdings for rent. Unlike the various unofficial enterprises of the period, it did not see small-holdings as simply a measure for the relief of urban unemployment. As an American student of the British system, Newlin Russell Smith, put it, "At last they were to assume permanently the landlord's risk, buy land and hold it, and rent it to suitable applicants in holdings of one to fifty acres. At last councils could compel the supply of land. They were to build buildings where necessary and, far beyond the buying and the building, they could borrow from national government funds (at rates of $3\frac{1}{2}$ per cent). Exchequer funds were also to be granted outright to the council's use. These grants were to be spent to find out the demand for small-holdings, advertise small-holdings, draw up detailed plans of buildings for and layout of small-holdings" and so on. The Board of Agriculture was given power to appoint commissioners who "were to stimulate the local demand where the county councils were farmer- or landlord-ridden and unwilling to assume the responsibility for providing small-holdings... Power and later funds, were provided to the Board of Agriculture to promote and capitalise the organisation of co-operative societies among smallholders."

It was in fact a very important piece of legislation and its effects were felt differently in different parts of the country ever since. There were places in the North or in the Fenlands where it catered for a long build-up of need. Interestingly enough, in spite of the philanthropists' concentration on Essex, this is not a county where its influence was much felt and it figures rather low in the statistics of holdings provided and families whose main source of income came from the statutory small-holding.

The First World War was far more influential. Not only did it provide a short-lived viability for Britain's declining agriculture and horticulture, but it left an aftermath of desire for a small-holding life. Lloyd George, as war-time Prime Minister, declared in a speech which, as Newlin Smith said, "epitomised, stimulated, and perhaps exploited" the hold of the land settlement idea. He said "There must be a scheme for settling the gallant soldiers and sailors on the land... The vast majority will return to their old occupations. But I am told that a good many of them who have been living an open-air life do not want to return to the close atmosphere of workshop and factory. If that is the case, they ought to have the opportunity of living on the land..."

It actually was the case. Land became available, in theory, on a scale never before known. The pre-war introduction of death duties and the slaughter of the inheritors in the First World War resulted in a situation when, to quote Howard Newby, "In four years between 1918 and 1922 England, in the words of a famous *Times* leader of the day, 'changed hands'. One quarter of the area of England was bought and sold in this hectic period of transaction, a disposal of land which was unprecedented since the dissolution of the monasteries in the sixteenth century."

Not much of it actually benefitted the ex-soldiers for whom the Land Settlement (Facilities) Act of August 1919 was intended. Its provisions, which ended in 1926, had not really worked, neither through county councils, nor directly from the Ministry of Agriculture, even though they included colonies with central farms attached, profit-sharing farms and co-operative marketing. Newlin Smith said that viewed either as a demobilisation measure or as a reward to heroes, it was not outstanding. "Of the millions demobilised only forty-nine thousand applied for small-holdings by December 1920, and only about one-third of these had received statutory small-holdings by December 1924."

All the same, "as a result of this war-induced land settlement, statutory small-holdings were more than doubled in number, and the number of houses on small-holding projects quadrupled... By 1924-25 the thirty thousand holdings of the combined pre-war and post-war estates had about eighty-two hundred houses upon them... A further thirty-six hundred of council's holdings were 'partially equipped', usually with buildings only. The remaining 60 per cent, or eighteen thousand, were bare land holdings without houses and buildings and were supplied close to the applicant's established residence."

This is a reminder that there were always plenty of people who gained part of their income from horticulture, or grazing or pig- and poultry-keeping, and the rest from regular, part-time or occasional jobs, who don't figure in the small-holding statistics. Something else that is not measured in the figures is what they and their families felt about their lives. This is something that I would like to learn from the survivors. It is worth remembering that the *normal* condition of pre-war rural England was one of poverty, decay and dereliction.

Just to stay within the Essex horizons it is worth recalling that Cecil Hewett, known to people here as the great authority on mediaeval timber building construction, was brought up in Laindon, and a Sunday paper account of his achievements tells how "His father, a wood machinist, fought on the Somme and must have been an interesting man; he and Cecil used to go for long walks in what was then the countryside, where, in the agricultural depression

71

of the 1930s, the old wooden farm machinery, the waggons and the carts, were lying about unused and open for examination."

It wasn't only agriculture that was depressed in the 1930s, and as always, here and in other countries, land settlement was seen as a partial remedy. This brings me to my final historical example, the Land Settlement Association, which was started in full consciousness of the absolute or relative failure of previous ventures of this kind and of the need to avoid more disappointments.

The LSA was conceived at a meeting in 1933 between the Prime Minister, Ramsay MacDonald, the Ministers of Agriculture and Labour, and representatives of the National Council for Social Service and the Society of Friends. It was born in the following year as a provident society constituted by these bodies and the Carnegie trustees, with a guarantee of matching money from the government to that raised privately and with the intention, it was announced, "to carry out an experimental scheme for the provision of smallholdings for unemployed persons, with financial assistance from the government."

Of the twenty-one estates set up before the war, two were in Essex, Yeldham, near Castle Hedingham, and Foxash at Ardleigh, not far from here. Yeldham was turned back into a single farm after the war. Foxash remained an LSA estate until 1983. It was originally a 700-acre site split between orchards and fifty-nine holdings of between four and seven acres.

The LSA was a kind of compulsory co-operative society (if that is not a contradiction in terms) in which the tenants were not members or voters. The element of compulsion was thought inevitable by the founders in order to overcome the universal problems of the small grower. "It was considered impractical to try and organise a voluntary system amongst what was essentially a group of strangers, and in an environment totally alien to their previous experience," while financial success depended on each grower making use of the central services.

Hardly had the survivors among the original tenants established themselves when war came. This brought full employment and a guaranteed demand for home-grown produce. Control of the association was taken over by the Ministry of Agriculture, and a new kind of settler came in: people with proven experience for whom the small-holding was either a chosen way of life, or else, in the well-worn phrase, "the first rung on the farming ladder." In the post-war years a series of committees of inquiry examined the Association, which was "rationalised" to meet modern marketing conditions. The estates were halved in number, those in the north and north-west were sold off. The mixed approach of poultry, pigs and vegetables was abandoned in favour of salad crops. Exactly like Tom Smith 85 years ago, each tenant found that the road to success was an increasing area of modern glasshouses. Incoming tenants or their spouses had to have agricultural experience as well as capital of their own. By 1970 it was reckoned that a new tenant needed £8,000, of which £2,000 was his or her own and the rest a loan from the Ministry. And by that year the average earnings of LSA tenants were well above the average agricultural wage. The Association, from its central office, adapted its activities to modern trends in retailing. It contracted directly with large multiple stores to supply a small range of salad crops — lettuces, tomatoes, celery and a few others. The demands of the big buyers dominated output.

Growers' incomes had become very chancy. Some estates were more successful than others, and even on the same estate some tenants were more skilful, more lucky or just more hardworking than others, or else had been able to invest more in glasshouses and equipment. And of course, the income represented a *family* wage, since being able to pick, trim, wash and package thousands of heads of celery in the early morning because Sainsbury's were having their Celery Week, depended on using the children and neighbours too.

The ten years before closure brought bad times. Tenants blamed a variety of factors. They blamed the huge increase in oil prices after 1973, the ever-increasing competition from imports, especially from Holland where small-holders benefit from subsidies (including one on the cost of fuel for heated greenhouses). Because of the national pooling of income between estates, the more successful growers blamed the less successful ones, especially those who left the Association with a mountain of bad debts. Most of all they blamed the organisation itself, for its high overheads and the rising standing charges which each tenant had to pay.

The Ministry commissioned two separate reports, one from the Central Council for Agricultural and Horti-cultural Co-operation and another from PA Management Consultants. The management report exonerated head office. Given the rules, it said, the costs and charges were reasonable. The marketing report echoed that of a much earlier inquiry headed by Professor M.J. Wise in 1963, which had concluded that the element of compulsion was the root of all the members' troubles.

Just before parliament broke up for Christmas in 1982, Peter Walker announced the demise of the LSA. The Ministry cut off both long-term and short-term finance, and tenants were given the opportunity to buy their holdings at what was said to be half the current market price. In January 1984 former Essex tenants together with others from the Newbourn estate in Suffolk formed a new marketing co-operative Home Grown Salads, with its head office in Canterbury, the base of Home Grown Fruits. Other former LSA tenants formed other co-operatives.

In keeping with the ideology of the present govern-ment, they have all to sink or swim in an increasingly competitive international market.

What are the lessons of a century of support for land settlement? I don't know, but I am confident that there are people in this audience who do, and I am hoping to hear from them.

References

[1] Martin Wiener: *English Culture and the Decline of the Industrial Spirit 1850–1980* (C.U.P., 2nd edition, 2004).

[2] Dennis Hardy and Colin Ward: *Arcadia For All* (Mansell, 1984, Five Leaves, 2003).

[3] Dennis Hardy: *Alternative Communities in Nineteenth Century England* (Longman, 1979).

[4] Peter Kropotkin: *Fields, Factories and Workshops* (new ed., Freedom Press, 1998).

[5] William Booth: *In Darkest England and the Way Out* (Forgotten Books, 2010).

Regionalist Seeds Beneath the Centralist Snow

Address to the course directed by Kirkpatrick Sale on Bioregionalism: Organising communities according to natural formations not political boundaries, at Schumacher College, Devon, April 1992

If you are hardened attenders at conferences, symposia, colloquia and courses, you will be familiar with the person who barges in at the very end, and harangues you, arrogantly oblivious of the paths you have already travelled, the crude objections you have coped with, the thickets you have negotiated, the authorities you have cited. Above all, this cuckoo in your nest is ignorant of the personal rapport you have built up in your days together and the delicately constructed consensus you have achieved.

Ladies and gentlemen, I am that interloper, and you will just have to forgive me. I haven't until today, met Kirkpatrick Sale, nor read his book *Dwellers in the Land: The Bioregional Vision*.[1] But I have read his invaluable compendium *Human Scale*,[2] and I have an enjoyable feeling that I carry the same cultural luggage as him, deriving from the founding fathers of French geography, Elisée Reclus and Paul Vidal de la Blache, from the founding fathers of Russian anarchism, Michael Bakunin and Peter Kropotkin, and from the Scottish biologist Patrick Geddes with his concept of the Valley Section as the framework of Place, Work and Folk, — certainly a bioregional view, from the Garden City pioneer Ebenezer Howard, and from the brilliant synthesiser of many of their ideas, Lewis Mumford, the most influential of the founders of the Regional Planning Association of America.

You and Kirkpatrick, and me too, can find some comfort from the fact that the ideas and approaches you have been exploring belong to a tradition of regionalist thinking. They haven't been plucked out of the Devon air. It was encouraging to me that when our best-known regional geographer, Professor Peter Hall, brought out his recent book *Cities of Tomorrow*[3] which he subtitled as "an intellectual history of urban planning and design in the twentieth century", he chose to stress the anarchist argument for small-scale human societies based on the ecology of their regions, and the view of the geographer Paul Vidal de la Blache that "the region was more than an object of survey; it was to provide the basis for the total reconstruction of social and political life." For Vidal, he explains, the region, not the nation, which "as the motor force of human development; the almost sensual reciprocity between men and women and their surroundings, was the seat of comprehensible liberty and the mainspring of cultural evolution, which were being attacked and eroded by the centralised nation-state and by large-scale machine industry." And Hall argued that:

> many, though by no means all, of the early visions of the planning movement stemmed from the anarchist movement, which flourished in the last decades of the nineteenth century and the first years of the twentieth... The vision of these anarchist pioneers was not merely of an alternative built form, but of an alternative society, neither capitalist nor bureaucratic–socialistic: a society based on voluntary co-operation among men and women, working and living in small self-governing communities.

But of course, while the pioneering advocates of town and country planning saw it as a great popular movement of citizens, what it became in practice was two things. Firstly, a profession with its hierarchies and its body of theory, subject to continual changes in fashion, and the pretence that it was a purely technical, value-free, scientific operation, not a matter of political, social and financial controversy. Secondly, a branch of government, local and national, since elected councillors sit on

77

planning committees, and since a Minister, with a vast, permanent department of government employees, makes decisions both on huge issues of policy and on individual cases. This person is the Secretary of State for the Environment, appointed by the Prime Minister of the ruling party. In the title of your conference, Kirkpatrick speaks of "organising communities according to natural formations not political boundaries." He is right, of course, in drawing attention to the fact that these do not coincide. If we raised the matter with the Secretary of State, he would brush it aside, and refer us to another government body, the Boundaries Commission. This is the body charged with re-drawing those political boundaries, largely in order to accommodate shifts in the settlement patterns of the human population to ensure some kind of parity in numbers. It makes its recommendations sparingly for several reasons, one of which is that changes of this kind are unpopular. Every individual person develops a cognitive map of the locality in which they live: they do have a notion of the limits of their parish and of their region. These may or may not be bioregions.

Now without knowing what kind of consensus you may have reached in your discussions over the last two weeks, I'm sure that you must have thought about how and whether it can be fed into the actual political and administrative machinery that governs land-use planning in this country. So I have a duty to say something about the structure of local government, a topic which carries a high boredom quotient, and one on which I am not any kind of authority. Just for brevity, I will raise a series of points.

1. There are countries where local government, in the form of city states and their rural hinterland, is much older than central state authority. Despite its ancient regions, Britain is not one of these. And the fact that settlements claim that they were established by royal charter some time after 1066 doesn't alter the fact that

the powers and scope of councils are severely limited and controlled by central government. It created them and can abolish them, as it did with the Metropolitan County Councils in 1986. Local government dates from the 1880s when county councils, based on ancient boundaries, were founded, together with borough councils, rural and urban district councils, county boroughs and the confirmation of powers which city councils had already acquired. The present system dates from 1974, the result of years of discussion and reporting. In England and Wales we have county and district councils, Scotland has regional and district councils. There were plenty of new boundaries and new names. It gave rise to huge expense and huge resentment, but the one thing that most people couldn't bear was further change, especially as many citizens still have the vaguest notion as to which authority is responsible for which local service. In matters of planning, both district and county councils are involved, while parish councils are consulted. When planning matters are disputed, the final ruling is made by central government which may uphold or overrule the decisions of local planning authorities.

2. Change is in the air again. One interpretation of central policy since 1979 is that it has been a long vendetta of central government against local councils, by reducing their incomes, and by taking away control of various services. Personally I am not a lover of local authorities, but I am much more worried about the centralisation of everything. You do need to be reminded that now there have been changes in Romania and Albania, the United Kingdom is the most centralised nation in Europe. Much more power is devolved in Germany, Spain and Italy, and, contrary to legend, France, than in this country.

   The major political parties each offer further change. Labour promises regional assemblies. The

Conservatives propose to iron out anomalies and have a unitary, rather than a binary system of local government, based, so it is said, on the district councils, possibly enlarged. However, the coming election is not going to be fought on these issues, except perhaps in Scotland. I don't believe that any party is proposing to surrender the key and absolute power over revenue-gathering held by the Treasury.

3. I must now turn to the regionalist element in British planning, in terms not of the area you have examined, "the Dart-watershed bioregion" but of much larger entities, like the South-West of England. The first generation of British planners, like say Sir Patrick Abercrombie, or in Scotland, Sir George Pepler, were very heavily influenced by the regional approach they had absorbed from Sir Patrick Geddes, and from Sir Ebenezer Howard. (I stress that they were all made knights, just to emphasise that their opinions had been absorbed into established opinion and attitudes.)

However, it was not until 1965, when, responding to regionalist propaganda from bodies like the Town and Country Planning Association, central government instituted ten regional councils "designed to monitor the problems and potential of each of the nation's regions." Since it affects an individual known to people here, I will quote from Dennis Hardy's recent book *From New Towns to Green Politics*[4] on this experience:

"Although the lack of real powers for the new councils, and failure to integrate their work with mainstream governmental policy-making was a source of concern, the Town & Country Planning Association held back criticism until the system had a chance to prove itself. Three years later, however, a leading member of the executive, Maurice Ash, resigned from the South West Regional Planning Council, on the grounds that the government had sacrificed the benefits of planning urban regions for the wider goal of 'regional balance'. The policy of increasing aid for outlying regions, as a substitute for a comprehensive regional policy, was roundly condemned. 'I find it lamentable and unnecessary,' concluded Ash, 'that a policy of indiscrimiaate aid to development areas, not posited-upon points of growth, should so soon have brought about this conflict of regionalisms. We have seen a false dawn.'"

Ash had tried, and failed, in his own eyes, to seize the chance of making an impact on policy through accepting a place on this advisory body. Years later, the incoming Conservative government of 1979, believing that the planning system was a constraint on enterprise, abandoned any specific regional policy and abolished the Regional Economic Planning Councils altogether. But of course the issues remained, and there was a quiet turnaround in government attitudes. Early in 1989 the Department of the Environment sent out a circular to local authorities inviting them to contribute to the preparation of the regional planning guidance that central government proposed to issue.

Now you and I are likely to be sceptical, to say the least, about the value of central government's guidance on regional issues, but it will presumably shape the policies of local county planning authorities, who in turn have been submitting joint regional strategies from bodies with names like the South West Regional Planning Conference and the West Midlands Forum of Local Authorities, after opening the exercise to public discussion and consultation. If you take seriously the issues you have been working on during your conference, it is important to know what is going on in official circles. Just in case there are people here who are as ignorant as I am in this area, I have photocopied for everyone an able article from the January issue of the TCPA journal *Town and Country Planning* by Tim Marshall, with the title "How Green is your region?" He begins with the question you will all ask: "As regional planning edges its way back into some form of acceptability — albeit in the form of non-statutory guidance — how far has the work of the informal regional conferences and forums reflected the groundswell of environmental concern?" Having said this, and without letting you off the task of reading his account, I have to quote to you one of his conclusions, which is relevant to your discussions. Tim Marshall concludes that "So far, despite much progress, it is clear that regional planning has not been able to tackle a fundamental analysis of the main bases of life in each region. This would involve looking extensively at the implications of all existing and proposed development (industrial, residential, transport) for each of the life-support systems or components — air, water, soil, minerals and fuels."

You and I are likely to be very sceptical about governmental gestures towards regional planning, about the strategies that consortia of councils submit to the Department of the Environment, about the consultation process that precedes them, and about the Regional Planning Guidance that the Department then issues. In terms of bio-regions, of Patrick Geddes' Valley Section, we may see a polarisation between local Boosterism on the one hand: the urge to see every valley become a Silicone Glen of new sources of employment; and of local Nimbyism on the other, that all-too-common attitude in rural England that says, in effect, "We bought our way into this delightful unspoiled place five years ago, and live on income earned elsewhere, but no-one else should do so because *they* would upset the delicate ecological balance of the area, thus causing an environmental disaster."

The penalty attached to serious advocacy of bio-regionalism includes an obligation to monitor, and even perhaps to participate in, the processes by which official regional policies are reached. It also needs a quite sophisticated understanding that government is a short-term activity and that the long-term vision implied by the idea of planning has a low priority in the hierarchy of government, whether local or national. Planners, whether professional or amateur, and whether good or bad, are far less influential in policy than the grand claims they make would imply.

4. There is also a European dimension. Most of us are bored by the politics of the European Community, and this is understandable, considering that we only hear about silly directives from the bureaucrats of Brussels about what vegetable seeds may be sold, or misrepresentations of the meaning of the word "federalism", which as you will know, has an interpretation elsewhere which is quite different from the one presented here. I don't follow the European debate, but I'm not a patriot either. I thoroughly support the slogan 'Think globally: act locally' and I observe that within the various pan-European assemblies there is a current urging the importance of a Europe of the Regions, and arguing that the nation state was a feature of the 16th to 19th centuries that will not have a useful future in the 21st century. They claim that the forthcoming nature of administration in a federated Europe is a link between, say, Calabria, Wales, Andalusia, Aquitaine or Saxony, as regions (not necessarily bio-regions), seeking their economic, ecological or cultural identity which had been lost in their incorporation in nation states where the centre of gravity is elsewhere.

The advocates of a united Europe have developed a doctrine which they call "subsidiarity", arguing that decisions should not be taken by the supranational institutions of the EC, nor by national governments, but preferably by regional or local levels of administration. The principle has been adopted, in its *Charter for Local Self-Government,* to, as it says, "formalise commitment to the principle that government functions should be carried out at the lowest level possible and only transferred to higher government by consent."

These words are significant, since they imply what I have to call the Swiss system of confederation, with the supremacy of the *Commune,* whatever its size and whether urban or rural, as the decision-making unit of social organisation, linked where necessary by the *Canton* for wider purposes, and with a purely administrative *Federal Council.* I need hardly add, just as Gandhi remarked: "For me, India is an idea, not a geographical expression", so to me Switzerland is an idea, and not what actually happens today in that confederation of states.

Now you might very well ask, "Does it matter what European politicians debate at our expense?" One reason why it does matter is that, whoever wins elections here, the fact that the European Community disposes of huge funds derived from member governments, affects the future of local government here. It already does. You will have heard that a grant from the European Community to an area devastated by pit closures has been held up by the Commissioner as the British government proposes to put the sum into general revenue and not to direct it to the place involved. Central government will have to yield. I need to quote to you from yet another article in the January issue of *Town and Country Planning,* a study by Janice Morphet of the consequences of the Maastrict Treaty, under the heading "The irresistible regional imperative". She reports that "The methods of allocating EC funding are in the process of reform. Soon, all funds will be operated on a regional basis... This recognition of the regional imperative could be the driving force of local government re-organisation. Whatever happens, EC funds will be allocated between regions, of which there will be twenty-four in the UK (although it has not as yet been possible to obtain a plan of these regions)." Think of the implications of this. While you have been exploring bio-regionalism, the European Community, though not your county or district council, has made its own assessment of what economic regions in Britain are. And I need to quote a further passage from Janice Morphet's assessment. She says that:

> Central government *must* involve local government much more openly in the discussions which take place in Brussels, and they have to be more honest. The Environmental Protection Act and the forthcoming new Green Bill are among many pieces of legislation being promoted in the UK to keep us in conformity with European requirements. Why are local authorities and interest groups not involved more in the preparation of new directives and the lobbying which accompanies their development? This is how policy is made. What is *more* likely to occur in the near future, as a result of Maastricht, is that local authorities will now have direct links with the Commission. The local authority associations have at last attempted to seize their chance, and look as if they have headed off the move from the civil service to represent local government on the new Consultative Council of Regional and Local Authorities. Thus Maastricht could open a whole new lease of life for local authorities just as local government re-organisation seems to be threatening a reduction of their role... Local government could emerge as a strong alternative to Whitehall.

Now you could study the newspapers and have no realisation that the British government at Maastricht was putting its signature to decisions which have big implications for your considerations of the last two weeks on bioregionalism. We can see it as one more indication of the fatuity of government, or of the meaninglessness of international resolutions.

But we can also see you people as explorers in depth of issues that are right at the centre of international debate, going home with the resolve to insert the priorities that you have hammered out for yourselves into the regionalist debate that is being conducted under the surface in the bigger world outside. Maybe you are the seed beneath the snow.

References

[1] Kirkpatrick Sale: *Dwellers in the Land* (University of Georgia, 2000).

[2] Kirkpatrick Sale: *Human Scale* (New Catalyst, 2007).

[3] Peter Hall: *Cities of Tomorrow* (Wiley-Blackwell, 2002).

[4] Dennis Hardy: *From New Towns to Green Politics* (Routledge, 1991).

Whose Land Is It Anyway?

Talk at the occupied Guinness site at Wandsworth in South London, on 8 May 1996

Naturally it is exciting for me to be talking to you in a building which did not exist three days ago, on a vast urban site which has been empty for years. You have asked me to say something about the history of squatting, since it is actually fifty years since the biggest occupations of derelict land/buildings in British history.

It seems to me that squatting can be seen as *ideological* or *pragmatic*. What I mean by this is that when Winstanley and the Diggers settled on land at Walton-on-Thames in Surrey in 1649, they were ideologists, dramatising a century of unauthorised encroachments, pushed on, as Christopher Hill noted, "by land shortage and pressure of population." Similarly, when in September 1969 squatters occupied a former royal residence, No 144 Piccadilly in central London, with a banner proclaiming Proudhon's slogan "Property is Theft", they were ideologists, dramatising the scandal of homelessness in a city where at the time acres of useable housing was empty, waiting for vast redevelopment proposals and road-building, which in the event never happened. We need to be reminded of the finding by Dr Graham Lomas that in London, by 1975, more fit houses had been destroyed than had been built since the second world war.

There have always been pragmatic squatters, relying on the distant and absentee property-owners, to allow them the occupation of premises by default. The last thing they desired was publicity and the thing they most desired was a rent-book and security of tenure. You will know that the term "Squatters' Rights" is a popular term for the complicated case-law of Adverse Possession, which means, broadly-speaking, that if you have had unchallenged occupation of land or buildings for twelve years, you can claim ownership.

We have a continuous history of squatting in the margins of history. A Victorian historian of Windsor Castle observed that at one time paupers had squatted in many of the towers. In the early ninteenth century an apple-seller called Ann Hicks annexed a portion of Hyde Park at the east end of the Serpentine. Her shanty was known as the White House and was steadily improved. An admirer, Katherine Lloyd, explained that "From a stall with an awning, a lock-up shop was evolved. Then a small back enclosure appeared including four walls with windows and a door. The height of the building was next increased, and under the excuse of repairing the roof a chimney was provided. The next step was to get a hurdle erected to prevent the curious from peeping in at the window. The fence by degrees was moved outwards, until a fair amount of space was enclosed. At this stage the authorities intervened and secured possession of the domain of Ann Hicks who was granted a small allowance."

However, I have to turn to the period at the end of the second world war. It started in 1945 with what was known as the Vigilante campaign which spread from Brighton to other seaside towns like Hastings and Southend. Committees of, largely, ex-servicemen, under cover of night, installed homeless families and their furniture in unoccupied houses — usually successfully, since no action could be taken to evict them once they were in, until the usually absentee property-owners could initiate legal proceedings against them.

In the following year the campaign grew because of the anomaly of the emptying-out of hundreds of army and air force camps during the worst housing shortage the country had known. The first of the 1946 squatters was James Fielding, a cinema projectionist from Scunthorpe who, desperate for somewhere to live so that he could keep his job, moved on May 8 with his family, into the former officers' mess of an unoccupied anti-aircraft camp. As soon as the news of their action spread around the town, other young couples in a similar predicament moved into the other huts and the first of the new squatter colonies was born. Two other camps in Lincolnshire were seized, and this was followed by the occupation of several camps around Sheffield. At Sheffield, settlers formed a Squatters' Protection Society and linked up with the pioneer squatters at Scunthorpe.

These events were rapidly followed by the seizure of hundreds of camps everywhere in Britain. The authorities, who at first disclaimed any responsibility for the squatters — passing the buck from one department to another — were forced to recognise the occupations, and local authorities were instructed to turn on water and electricity supplies. Later in the year the Ministry of Works, which had previously declared itself "not interested", found it possible to offer the Ministry of Health (then the department responsible for housing) 850 former service camps.

The government announced on 11 October 1946 that 1,038 camps in England and Wales had been occupied by 39,535 people, and on 5 September it was stated that four thousand people had squatted in Scotland. Since the government could not destroy the movement, it tried to absorb it, and expressed itself confident that the settlers would "see reason" and "move out when the situation had been explained to them." On Saturday 14 September, the Minister of Health, Aneurin Bevan, just back from his holiday in Switzerland, instructed local authorities to cut off gas and electricity supplies to property under their control occupied by squatters.

But in fact, by this time, councils were already directing homeless people to occupy empty huts, where settlers were organising communal cooking and nursery facilities and forming a rota to stoke the boilers left behind by the armed forces. A very revealing report in a series called "How Are They Now?" appeared in the *News*

Chronicle for January 14 1947. The correspondent described a Lancashire camp:

> There are two camps within the camp — the official squatters (that is, people who have been placed in the huts after the first invasion) and the unofficial squatters (the veterans who have been allowed to remain on sufferance). Both pay the same rent of 10 shillings a week — but there the similarity ends. Although one would have imagined that the acceptance of rent from both should accord them identical privileges, in fact it does not. Workmen have put up partitions in the huts of the official squatters — and have put in sinks and numerous other conveniences. These are the sheep; the goats have perforce to fend for themselves.
>
> An interesting commentary on the situation was made by one of the young welfare officers attached to the housing department. On her visit of inspection she found that the goats had set to work with a will, improvising partitions, running up curtains, distempering, painting and using initiative. The official squatters on the other hand, sat about glumly without lifting a hand to help themselves and bemoaning their fate, even though they might have been removed from the most appalling slum property. Until the overworked corporation workmen got around to them they would not attempt to improve affairs themselves.

In October 1946, Aneurin Bevan sought to turn public feeling against the camp squatters by suggesting that they were "jumping their place in the housing queue", when in fact they were jumping out of the housing queue by moving into buildings which would not otherwise have been used for housing purposes. It took most of them years in fact to get into that "housing queue". Over a hundred families who in 1946 occupied a camp called Field Farm in Oxfordshire, stayed together, and over ten years later, in 1958-59, were rehoused in the new village of Berinsfield on the same site.

But meanwhile, as the camps began to fill, squatters turned to other empty buildings: houses, shops, mansions, disused school buildings, race tracks and a stadium were among the places occupied, and on August 26 1946 two Aberdeen hotels and on the 29th two big Glasgow hotels were seized, and later abandoned. The final and most spectacular phase of the campaign began in London on Sunday 8 September when the 148 former luxury flats of Duchess of Bedford House, Kensington, another block in Weymouth Street, Marylebone and big empty houses in Holland Park and Camden Hill were occupied. On the following day three more houses in Marylebone were taken over, and on the Tuesday sixty families entered Fountain Court, a block of flats in Victoria. On the Wednesday the flats at Abbey Lodge, Regents Park and the 630-room Ivanhoe Hotel in Bloomsbury were occupied. The tactics adopted by the police varied from day to day, from sympathy to threats, according to instructions from above.

The Communist Party, although a year earlier it had denounced the Brighton Vigilantes, was very active among the London squatters. So much so that people who had to rely on newspapers for their information assumed, and have assumed since, that the whole thing was a Communist stunt. The whole affair ended in the anti-climax of a "general evacuation" by the London squatters when a High Court injunction against them was granted. This was seen as the end of the squatting wave, though many of them were found accommodation of one kind or another by the London County Council, while the camp squatters settled down until they could find something better.

Needless to say, pragmatic squatting continued, especially as local councils acquired vast tracts of urban housing for eventual comprehensive redevelopment. It re-emerged as a public issue in 1968 thanks to two activists: Ron Bailey and Jim Radford. They were busy agitating about the failure of local authorities to comply with their statutory duty to the homeless, trying after long and bitter campaigns to draw public attention to conditions in hostels for homeless families in Kent and Essex and in the LCC area. By this time, as Bailey put it, "a squatting campaign was clearly on the cards; it only needed a spark to set it off," so they installed homeless families in unoccupied houses which had been publicly acquired and earmarked for demolition years later for eventual road improvements, car parking or municipal offices.

This outraged the local authorities, who responded violently. They used thugs described as "private investigators" as their agents to terrorise and intimidate the squatting families, and this was widely reported and photographed in the press and on television. This in turn drew public opinion towards support of the squatters, as did the policy of deliberately wrecking the interiors of empty houses just to keep the squatters out. I myself saw the way in which council employees smashed sinks and water closets, poured cement down the wastepipes and ripped out staircases so that even squatters could not settle there.

Bailey was commissioned by Penguin Books to write his account of the events in 1969, but his book was not published until 1973 because of lawsuits resulting from the activities of the so-called 'bailiffs' employed by one London council. When it did appear, his publishers omitted his concluding chapter which defended the squatters' movement both against those who oppose direct action from a constitutional point of view, and secondly against his critics on the allegedly revolutionary left. He remarked that, "In the squatters' movement I have worked with ordinary non-political people for admittedly small gains, and we achieved a large measure of success. Ordinary people acted and won; and ordinary people manage the houses in which they now live. So when councils offered to hand over houses we accepted these rather than fight over them unneccesarily." (Ron Bailey: "In Defence of Direct Action" *Wildcat* No 3, Nov 1974).

For what happened after the grotesque over-reaction of councils to the activities of the squatters, was that, ashamed of their mismanagement of empty housing they owned, they gladly entered into agreements for short-life housing co-ops, some of which, because of the changed climate of housing policy, have had a very long life. In London, some of the most successful housing co-ops have grown out of squatting groups. And in fact, a quarter of a century after his venture into the squatting world, Bailey dedicates his most recent book on the scandal of empty housing in a situation of homelessness, to the late Conservative chairman of the housing committee of the London Borough of Lewisham in 1968-71, in "admiration of the astonishing courage and vision he showed by entering into the first legal agreement with squatters in 1969"; and he adds that "As a result of his action, tens of thousands of homes that would otherwise have stayed empty have been brought back into use and hundreds of thousands of homeless people given new hope and dignity."

Local politicians may have come to agreements with squatters (and this is perhaps more evident in other European cities like Amsterdam, Hamburg and Copenhagen), but central government politicians of both major parties have been unremittingly hostile. Once they discovered that squatting was a civil, rather than a criminal offence, governed by legislation dating back to the year 1381, they set about changing the situation. The Law Commission responded in 1974 with a document on Criminal Law Offences of Entering and Remaining on Property, which was incorporated into legislation by the Criminal Law Act of 1977. This failed to deter this country's 50,000 or so squatters, and in practice, so has its Conservative successor, the infamous Criminal Justice Act of 1994.

During the preparation of the Labour government's legislation, surveys of squatters were undertaken by Mike Kingham and others, which demonstrated that typical squatters were not happy hippies, but people in desperate housing need. In preparation for the Criminal Justice Act twenty years later, the Home Office issued a Consultation Paper in which it stated that it "does not accept the claim that squatting results from social deprivation. Squatters are generally there by their own choice, moved by no more than self-gratification or an unreadiness to respect other people's rights." It also observed that cases of squatting "involving very young children were negligible".

Ron Bailey in his most recent book uses the latest available survey figures to show that the facts are very different. He finds that:

> About one third of squatting households contain children and this has been the case for over five years. Under Section 58 of the Housing Act 1985, all such families are statutorily homeless and so entitled to be accommodated by local authorities. This would often be bed and breakfast. The fact that they are squatting actually saves ratepayers vast amounts of money. Many other squatters need psychiatric help: since 1990 more than 28,000 hospital beds have been lost and only 5,000 residential places provided. Thus, many ill people have drifted into sleeping rough and squatting. In addition, currently 2,000 squatters are women escaping violent partners. Even more squatters are homeless single people for whom there is no statutory provision at all and for whom council waiting lists are meaningless. About one in twenty squatters (2,500 people) are ex-owner occupiers, evicted as they were unable to meet mortgage repayments. In conclusion, therefore, all the available evidence shows that squatters are homeless people in desperate housing need, often with other social problems such as mental illness or the need to escape violence and harassment. These are the people that the government is attempting to make into criminals.

The government ignored the representations of eminently reasonable people like Ron Bailey, who for thirty years has tried to seek some accommodation for the homeless in official policy, and, as you will know, the Criminal Justice Act incorporated an astonishing ragbag of legislation directed against the poor. Hence the important question: "Whose land is it anyway?"

Small Holdings

The Land is Ours Meeting at the Friends Meeting
House, 30 October 1997

In the 19th century, what was called The Land Question,
referring to the depopulation of the countryside and the
elimination of a British peasantry through the effect of
Enclosure Acts and the amalgamation of land holdings,
was endlessly raised in British politics. The importance of
the movement called The Land is Ours is precisely that it
is "a land-rights campaign for Britain," aiming to get
access to land back onto the political and social agenda in
the twenty-first century.

It has endless aspects. One is that of allotment
gardens, whose history has been told in a book by David
Crouch and me.[1] Another is that of access to the
countryside, the Freedom to Roam, which David had
intended to talk about tonight. Yet another is that of the
story of the plotlands and self-build housing, about which
I have written endlessly. Still another is that of what are
seen as Utopian communities resettling the land. Those
from the last century are described in a long-out-of-print
book by Dennis Hardy, *Alternative Communities in
Nineteenth Century England*.[2] If you take the trouble to
put your name down for it at your public library, the
library will eventually get it for you. It was all those
failed communities which led directly to twentieth
century government programmes of land settlement,
which I am to talk about tonight.

Books are important, and the 1890s saw a whole series
of books from different standpoints, tackling the land
question. The first was *In Darkest England and the Way
Out* (1890) by William Booth of the Salvation Army. The
second was very different: William Morris's *News from*

Nowhere (1890) about the post-industrial Britain of the twenty-first century. The third was Robert Blatchford's *Merrie England* (1893), the fourth was Leo Tolstoy's *The Kingdom of God is Within You* (1894), the fifth was Ebenezer Howard's *Tomorrow: A Peaceful Path to Real Reform* (1898) and the last was Peter Kropotkin's *Fields, Factories and Workshops* (1899). They led to endless experiment in places where land was cheap. Among those inspired by Tolstoy, a sole survivor celebrates its centenary in 1998. This is Whiteway in Gloucestershire, where the original settlers ceremonially burned the title deeds to the land to ensure that it was common to all. Inevitably this was challenged in the courts many decades later, and to the delight of most, the Chief Land Registry Tribunal ruled in 1955 that the colonists as a whole were the licensees of their land, with their monthly meeting held regularly since the formation of the colony, the licensor.

Whiteway survived through the tacit abandonment of the founders' faith in communal living, and in all these "Land Colonies" there were inevitable disagreements between rival versions of the Good Life. The Clousden Hill Free Communist and Co-operative Colony was established on a twenty-acre farm north of Newcastle-upon-Tyne in 1895. Its story was told by Nigel Todd in his book *Roses and Revolutionaries*.[3] The founder was a tailor, Frank Kapper, and this was a time when there was intense interest in the North-East in communal intensive horticulture. Kropotkin's articles and his at that time untranslated book *La Conquete du Pain*, as Todd explains,

> drew attention to the potential of applying artificial heating systems, greenhouses (or 'glass culture') and new fertilisers, to land cultivation. *Freedom* serialised an English translation, *The Conquest of Bread* in 1893-94, and coincidentally, the issue of reorganising agriculture within a democratic framework was raised in the North-East by the Co-operative Movement. In May 1894 the annual 'parliament' of the retail and

producer co-operatives — the Co-operative Congress — met at Sunderland, and on the agenda was a special paper dealing with 'Co-operative Agriculture'. This attracted the attention of anarchists who tended to have a soft spot for the co-operatives, seeing them as in essence voluntary, open associations of consumers and producers, successfully eliminating the private profit motive but hamstrung by bureaucratic leadership.

One of the debaters at this Congress in 1894 was a Londoner, John C. Kenworthy, who was urging delegates to support "voluntary co-operation on the land" rather than farms that just chanced to be owned by retail co-operative societies. He set up a fringe meeting on this theme, where Frank Kapper met the provider of capital for the purchase of Clousden Hill. This was William Key, who had been a seaman for twelve years, a miner for eight, and a publican and part-time insurance agent for another twelve, a background as improbable as that of Ebenezer Howard. Key and Kapper, anxious to do the right thing, wrote to Kropotkin (then living at Bromley in Kent, where English Heritage erected a Blue Plaque in 1989 to commemorate his residence) asking him to act as treasurer.

Kropotkin replied that, "I am the least appropriate person, as I was never able to keep accounts of my own earnings and spendings." He did, however, offer valuable advice for this and other community ventures:

> Kropotkin warned about dangers posed by the venture by insufficient funds, influxes of too many newcomers at times of prosperity in the colony, any failure to appreciate the need for hard work, and frustration that might arise out of the limited social life in small colonies... And he suggested that successful communities should be avoided in favour of combined efforts by independent families. Colonies should also reject internal authority structures.

He raised an issue of enormous relevance for community ventures: the situation of women. It was important, he reminded them:

to do all possible for reducing household work to the lowest minimum... In most communities this point was awfully neglected. The women and girls remained in the new society as they were in the old — slaves of the community. Arrangements to reduce as much as possible the amount of work which women spend in the rearing-up of children, as well as in household work are, in my opinion, as essential to the success of the community as the proper arrangements of the fields, the greenhouses, and the agricultural machinery. Even more. But while every community dreams of having the most perfect agricultural or industrial machinery, it seldom pays attention to the squandering of the forces of the house slaves, the women. (Todd, p.19)

The Clousden Hill venture aroused enormous interest and a stream of visitors and suffered an embarrassment of recruits, all of them anxious to change the rules: "day after day was spent in framing sets of rules", wrote one colonist. Nor did its eventual failure discourage other experiments. Each of those inspirational 'Back to the Land' books of the 1890s gave rise to a crop of horticultural experiments. Blatchford's *Merrie England* induced a Manchester printer, Thomas Smith, to change his occupation and to move with his family to eleven acres of heavy clay at Mayland, near Althorne, and to advertise for fellow colonists. It took him a long time to succeed, and to learn from experience, as Jan Marsh explained in *Back to the Land:*[4]

The most profitable produce at Mayland was tomatoes and other salad vegetables, and the earlier the crop the higher the price. Smith therefore steadily moved to cultivation under glass, producing strawberries, lettuce, tomatoes and even melons — all crops whose wholesale price was good even with small quantities. Gradually he acquired the knowledge and skill to make his holding into a thriving business. Later he published handbooks on intensive cultivation, although the picture they give of a scientifically-managed market garden with intensive manuring, acres of cold frame, carefully regulated cloches and a large packing shed is perhaps not the pastoral image Smith or others had before them when setting off back to the land.

Smith's rare success attracted the attention of an American philanthropist, Joseph Fels, founder of the Fels-Naptha Soap Company. George Lansbury, the Labour politician, had drawn him into collaboration with the Boards of Poor Law Guardians in London, under the provisions of the Unemployed Workmen's Act, which granted government money to various local unemployment committees to enable them to find work. With his aid Lansbury set up "labour colonies" at Hollesley Bay in Suffolk and at Laindon in Essex, where the work of 200 men, Lansbury claimed, "turned what was derelict land into orchards and gardens." He and Fels were preparing further schemes when a change of government early in 1906 brought a new president, John Burns, to the Local Government Board, who forbade the investment of public money in schemes for the resettlement of unemployed men on the land. Undeterred, Fels went ahead with the purchase of the 600-acre Nipsells Farm at Mayland, close to Thomas Smith's land, with the aim of providing "a long-term opportunity" rather than "short-term relief," with Smith as manager.

In 1912 a well-known advocate of small-holdings, F.E. Green, reported that this venture had not succeeded, "but then who could expect to find a French garden situated four and a half miles from a railway station a commercial success?" and he found that most of the smallholders were deeply in debt to Mr Fels. In *The Awakening of England* (1912) he described how:

> Many of these settlers came from Woolwich and other urban districts, and yet one cannot lay the blame altogether on the unfitness of the men. In my opinion, Mayland should never have been cut into five-acre fruit farms, but rather into thirty- or forty-acre stock-raising holdings. A life which presents to the townsman six months of digging heavy, dirty land, unrelieved by any

other winter occupation, is a sore test to the most ardent of earth lovers.

Green identified the difficulty that besets every small grower, whether individual or collective: that of effective marketing. He observed that,

> I was shown how the system of co-operative distribution in sending away the produce of all in bulk to market had been perfected, so I was told, 'up to the last button'; but what was the use of that when the produce was sent to Covent Garden on the chance of what it might fetch... In many instances produce hardly covered the cost of carriage... Co-operation merely perfected a method for making the fortunes of Covent Garden salesman. This might have been avoided had co-operative distributors come to the rescue of co-operative producers.

Ironically, it was the aftermath of the First World War that changed the aspiration for resettling the land from an experiment conducted by Tolstoyans, anarchists, simple-lifers and the Salvation Army, into a minor aspect of government policy.

The literature of the 1890s urging rural resettlement was astonishingly widely read. Blatchford's *Merrie England* had sold almost a million copies by the end of the century. And in 1908 the reforming Liberal government in its Small Holdings and Allotments Act had empowered county councils to acquire land and erect buildings with government funds, and rent holdings of from one acre to fifty acres. They were also enabled to promote and capitalise the organisation of co-operative societies among small-holders.

Ninety years later there are English counties where, because of that Act, the county council is the largest single landowner. Some counties have waiting lists of applicants for small-holdings, and as vacancies occur, face the dilemma of whether to create a new tenancy or to rent the holding to neighbouring tenants who claim that their fifty acres is too small for financial viability in the modern agricultural world. Other county councils, to raise revenue, sell holdings either to tenants or on the open market.

The impetus for settling families on the land after the First World War was, however, an aspect of that urban dream from the nineties that was reshaped for post-war aspirations. To meet the hopes of ex-servicemen and their families to make a living from the land a Land Settlement (Facilities) Act was passed in 1919, and its provisions ended in 1926. These included farm colonies with central farms attached, profit-sharing farms and co-operative marketing.

But the historian of these hopes reports that after the First World War:

> Of the millions demobilised, only forty-nine thousand applied for small-holdings and only about a third of these had received statutory holdings by December 1924... All the same, as a result of this war-induced land settlement, statutory small-holdings were more than doubled in number, and the number of houses on small-holding projects quadrupled... By 1924-25 the thirty thousand holdings of the combined pre-war and post-war estates had about eighty-two hundred houses upon them... A further thirty-six hundred of council's holdings were 'partially-equipped', usually with buildings only. The remaining 60 per cent, or eighteen thousand, were bare land holdings without houses and buildings and were supplied close to the applicant's established residence. (Smith, 1946, p.109)

In Scotland the issue of resettling ex-servicemen on the land was given additional impetus by historical circumstances. The 'Clearances' of the crofters in the Highlands and Islands had left appalling grievances which had not been rectified by the Crofting Act of 1886, which controlled rents and gave security of tenure, but did not reinstate the descendants of the evicted. In the period leading up to the First World War there had been a series of widely-publicised land raids. The historian Leah Leneoan explains that recruiting propaganda promised men who enlisted voluntarily that they would get land on their return. Those who fought and survived and wanted holdings were widely considered to deserve them.[5]

About 90 per cent of the land acquired in Scotland for land settlement between 1919 and 1930 was in the crofting counties, constituting about 60 per cent of the 2,536 holdings created, largely in an attempt to fufil "the long-standing cultural and political aspirations of the crofting population." (Todd, p.129). In England, as provision for ex-service families dwindled, the Religious Society of Friends, popularly known as the Quakers, sought to find ways of alleviating the hardships endured by unemployed miners. By 1935 it had persuaded the government to match the funds from other sources and initiate the Land Settlement Association, specifically for the relief of unemployment, and based on collective marketing for the families involved.

As sites around the country were bought, a charact-eristic LSA landscape emerged, recognisable even today in places disposed of by the LSA long before its final closure. There was a small home farm, usually the original farmstead, occupied by the supervisor or advisers, with central buildings for the grading and packing of produce, and beyond it about forty holdings of around four to eight acres, depending on the original assumptions about horticulture or stock-rearing as the basic activity. The tenants' houses, each with a small front garden, were built when possible on existing roads. Where necessary, new access roads were developed on a grid-iron layout.

Close to the dwellings were glasshouses, pig sheds and chicken-houses, followed by a patch for fruit and vegetable cultivation, and beyond that an area designed to be ploughed and harvested together with neighbouring plots. Sometimes there was also a large-scale orchard.

It was a landscape that resembled, if anything, that of the plotlands, which in some districts, like the Selsey Peninsula in West Sussex, were contiguous. The Second World War both denied the LSA its triumphs and spared it the problems of its failures. For when established horticulturists were already bankrupt, it was not surprising that unemployed families would not do any better. Those settlers who had failed to adapt to the growers' life moved back to their home regions, where suddenly, through the magic of war, mining and heavy industry had again become important. Food production too became a national imperative and the LSA fell under the direct control of the Ministry of Agriculture.

Post-war policy was to restrict applicants for holdings to people with proven farming experience and with access to enough capital to maintain the holder and the family until they were self-supporting. In the 1960s the Ministry appointed a committee chaired by Professor M.J. Wise to report both on smallholdings established by county councils and on those of the LSA. He concluded that the concept of the Association's estates as "the first step in the farming ladder" was no longer relevant, and that its role as an experimenter in agricultural co-operation had not been fulfilled, since its board was appointed by government and not by the tenants, and since they themselves were constrained by involuntary contractual obligation.

Meanwhile, the pattern of retailing in Britain was rapidly changing. The concept of local greengrocers and fruiterers buying in the nearest wholesale market, dominated by Covent Garden in London, was being replaced by direct purchasing by multiple chain-stores making their own deals with suppliers for high street supermarkets and out-of-town hypermarkets, with a high degree of pre-packaging and standardisation.

The LSA took the best available advice and contracted with the large multiple stores to supply a small range of salad crops in vast quantities. By the early 1970s

103

earnings were well above the average agricultural wage, but the late 1970s brought hard times to tenants. The Ministry's decision to close down the LSA was announced as Parliament went into recess in December 1982. The decision covered the ten remaining estates, comprising 3,900 acres with 530 tenants who were to be allowed to purchase their holdings at half the current market price. In what was known as the *annus mirabilis* of British farming, since farmers' incomes rose by forty per cent, it was found that up to a quarter of LSA tenants were in receipt of the social security Family Income Supplement.

There were messy law suits successfully getting a large out-of-court settlement from the Ministry. One Suffolk estate at Newbourn formed a new co-operative to recapture their market but were defeated by cheaper imports, and by 1994 it was reported that:

> Large areas where once a thriving community of families worked the land now looks like a bomb site. Acres of glasshouses stand idle. Clearing the glass costs £10,000 an acre, and with 25 to 30 acres of glass on the LSA site, this means a £250,000-plus bill. Growers want to sell up, but the council, in pursuit of its planning policy has banned any new building, and wants the site to retain its horticultural character. One grower for 17 years at Newbourn remarked that 'There's just no future in horticulture: it is obsolete, and we can no longer make a living at it. They want our holdings to be left as museum pieces, but without the curator's wages.'

This is the sad, muted and ironical end of the longest-lasting and largest-scale venture in enabling low-income people to earn a livelihood producing food in modern rural England. And in terms of access to land, there is a tacit conspiracy to exclude the poor, disguised as a concern for the environment. The campaign called The Land is Ours is very significant because it challenges all the conventional wisdom of rural England.

References

[1] David Crouch and Colin Ward: *The Allotment: Its Landscape and Culture* (Five Leaves, 1994/97).

[2] Dennis Hardy: *Alternative Communities in Nineteenth Century England* (Longman, 1979).

[3] Nigel Todd: *Roses and Revolutionaries* (People's Publications, 1986).

[4] Jan Marsh: *Back to the Land* (Quartet, 1982).

[5] Leah Leneoan: *Fit for Heroes* (Aberdeen U.P., 1989).

The Green Personality

Leicester Secular Society, Secular Hall, Humberstone Gate, Leicester 21 March 1999

It's a pleasure for me to be in this historic building, because I am one of those people who, before even knowing what the words meant, was a secularist and a rationalist with no urge to join any religious faith. I am, in fact, an anarchist, an opponent of the principle of authority, advocating a self-organising society based on voluntary co-operation. Political ideologies of the right, the left and the centre have had to adapt themselves to our new perceptions of the depletion of the planet's resources, the destruction of its atmosphere, and of the limits to global economic growth. From an anarchist standpoint, the green slogan "Think globally, act locally" is an admirable guide to conduct.

And indeed, when the famous book *Fields, Factories and Workshops*[1] by the most widely read anarchist propagandist, Peter Kropotkin, was reprinted in 1919, it was prefixed by a note explaining that "It pleads for a new economy in the energies used in supplying the needs of human life, since these needs are increasing and the energies are not inexhaustible."

This was an immensely acute comment, as you will see if you look for a similar recognition of the limits to growth in the literature of the following fifty years, for ecological awareness to seep into the general consciousness. However, his remark is eighty years old, and a whole series of people in different generations have sought to adopt a greener or more ecologically viable mode of life.

Now, of course, all through history there have been people urging us to reduce our demands on the economy or on the planet, very often from a religious motivation. Most religions include the injunction that we should sell all that we have and give to the poor, even though most of their adherents, like the rest of us, have managed to avoid following this advice.

But today the situation is different. We have a vast literature seeking to persuade us to reduce our demands on the world's resources in the interests both of future generations and of social justice. One recent example is the new book from Friends of the Earth, discussed by Shannon Little in the December 1998 issue of the *New Humanist*.[2] This report on *Britain's Share in a Sustainable Future* warns us, he notes, that "The world's richest twenty per cent consume eighty per cent of the world's resources. Using the United States and India as stark examples, the US owns 150 times as many cars as India per capita, as well as using 400 times as much wood pulp and three times as much water." And the authors "also note that the global economy exacerbates environmental destruction by allowing consumerist societies to take advantage of resources from around the world, in a persisting colonial system. Furthermore, measures of consumption and economic growth ignore costs to human well-being, which are particularly high in southern countries."

We are all familiar with similar observations on the global effects of the rich world's depletion of resources. Very importantly, the existence of poverty in the rich nations is recognised by the authors of the new FOE book. Quite often the moralists of sustainability ignore this, but these particular authors remark:

> If we fail to restore or create social justice in our communities in the UK, then whatever economic and environmental progress we make towards sustainability will be undermined, in the short-term by the costs of inequality, and in the longer term by the lack of social cohesion that results from inequality.

These authors also, as Shannon Little makes clear, "dismiss the Gross Domestic Product as a measure of economic growth, as it ignores human capital and well-being." And he comments that Friends of the Earth does not take an austere viewpoint of zero consumption, but rather has the "fundamental assumption that everyone should have access to a fair share of the resources and opportunities they need to live a pleasant and fulfilling life." He also cites their interesting comment that "additional income increases a sense of well-being for only the poorest fifth of the population."

This last point is remarkably interesting, and I have no idea how the researchers reached it. It is however immediately apparent to you and me through old sayings like "Money doesn't bring happiness", or through the law that is known by economists as "diminishing marginal utility", meaning that every additional CD that we buy, reduces the benefit we get from the 55 CDs we already own, or the 120 tapes, or the 200 LPs, quite apart from all the other items of recording that we own.

But we also know that deliberate government policy over the past twenty years has increased the number of fellow-citizens living in poverty, and that this is reflected in statistics of health and malnutrition, as well as in those for family breakdown, domestic violence and every kind of expensive misery. They suffer, not from the diminishing marginal utility of the affluent, but from an increasing marginality from the rest of society, pressed home on them by government policy since 1979 under governments of both political complexions.

During the Second World War, Noël Coward, whose centenary we have been celebrating recently, sent a postcard of some luxury liner, with the message, "We may all be on a sinking ship, but that's no reason why some of us shouldn't travel first class."

This whimsical approach was turned into government policy in this country in 1979, under the influence of free market ideologists, so that the rich became richer and the poor poorer. A current, devastating book about urban life today, *Dark Heart* by Nick Davies,[3] is devoted to reports on the making of the new underclass in Britain today. Davis comments on the way that,

> The economic reality is that there are several million British workers whose labour power is no longer needed. Their role as labour has been stolen away by new technology, by the availability of much cheaper labour in Asia and South America, by the drive for higher productivity. They are in the deepest sense redundant. Looking at them from a strictly economic point of view, these former workers and their families are worthless. More than that, they are an expensive burden — at least they will be if they are to be properly housed and clothed and fed, if they are to be given decent schools and hospitals. So, why bother?

He argues that the commercialisation of human relations has handed us over to "greed and selfishness and a ruthless self-indulgence — to the values at the dark heart of Britain", and that one government after another has endorsed these attitudes. He adds that, "Every time a government minister from any party stands up and declares war on the welfare state, every time some respected thinker jeers at the idea of equality, or contrives a case for stripping the poor of yet more benefits, they give a cloak of credibility to this hardness."

Now, especially as I am both old and poor, I know all too well that if green attitudes are imposed on us by law, the poor will be penalised while the affluent won't even notice. This was the result of the imposition of VAT on domestic fuel by the last government, in pursuing the intergovernmental agreements decided at Rio in 1992. For this reason and all the others associated with fuel efficiency, it was reported by the housing historian Alison Ravetz that:

> Energy is quite simply rationed by price, and, as in all other departments of life, the poor pay more for less. Tenants pay more per kilowatt-hour than owner-occupiers, and as a proportion of household income, those

with the lowest incomes spend roughly twice as much as the national average on their energy and fuel.[4]

Once you pause and think about it, you realise that in one area of life after another, the effect of introducing green values by legislation is to put even greater burdens on poor people. I could show this to be true in endless aspects of life. The affluent get better for less in everything from banking to motoring. Maybe the exception is food. The poor get junk food at junk prices, while the affluent can buy high quality organically-produced food at high prices from specialist outlets, or even in the hypermarket when the demand is there. In response, of course, the children of the affluent buy junk food at high prices, just like the poor but spending more.

I've said enough to indicate that in the uphill task of the greening of modern British society, social justice seems more important to me than the imposition of green priorities as decided by all those government spokesmen jetted into the gated condominiums of the ruling elite in Rio. I find something quite hilarious about governments of any colour telling their citizens how to be green.

But nor do I enjoy the company of those green advocates who like to play the game of green theology. We have all heard about those mediaeval theologians or Talmudic scholars who would argue about the precise number of angels who could dance on the head of a pin. If I switch off a light out of an ordinary sense of economy, they urge me to consider that because the starting device of a fluorescent lamp uses more power than running the lamp, maybe I would be greener if I left the lamp running all day. Similarly, when I take the bottles, cans or paper for recycling, friends will buttonhole me to ask whether I have thought that my journey to the bin, and the infinitely longer journey that my rubbish takes in order to be recycled, makes the whole recycling exercise ludicrous.

No, I haven't thought about these theological issues, nor whether I use less or more energy in using a manual

110

typewriter and the postal system, than in using a word-processor, e-mail or the Internet. I don't care.

In one sense I *do* care. It does matter to me that my local council has to dispose of my rubbish, and that even when I weed out of this the organic or recyclable bits, most of the rubbish *I* produce is some form of packaging, made only because if the item I wanted to buy was unwrapped, I might have stolen it. In vain I protest my innocence.

And in another sense I do care. In my lessons about elementary economics I learned that the aim of capital is to do away with labour, and I have watched this happening all my life, but much more recently, I have watched every conceivable public service employer regarding it as a triumph if they could provide a livelihood for fewer people. Everyone here has watched this decline in service whether from the post office or the water, gas, or electricity supplier.

In a climate of mass unemployment, we are obliged to ask why the modern equivalent of those people who once provided a service are really better off when they have no job and are regarded by government and our fellow citizens as a drag on the economy if they just want to stay alive.

My own interpretation of greenness makes me value people providing an actual and personal service to their fellow-humans. But as market ideology dominates us to an increasing extent, it isn't only the old chap who made sure the taps worked, but nurses and teachers who are seen as less preferable than anyone with a job in the market, even if they are selling goods or services which you and I would be better off without. The fact that the national economy can't afford useful people while profitable exploiters are said to be part of the nation's prosperity, tells me that official economics are nonsense.

As an unsuccessful propagandist, I have not learned how to change the habits of our fellow citizens. In 1990 I was asked by the anarchist publishers, Freedom Press, to write a book about transport. This was not an easy task since anarchists tend to prescribe an ideal world where life is simple, rather than discussing the conflicts of interests and desires in the complex world in which we actually live.

I have even heard it said that in an anarchist society transport would not be an issue or a problem because happy and contented people would enjoy life without mobility. But I can remember hearing the American thinker Lewis Mumford talking about the obvious *liberating* effect of modern personal mobility, calling it the *freedom to go.* So I used that phrase for the title of my book, with the subtitle, *After the Motor Age.*[5] It was published in 1991 and was (I am sorry to say) very Anglocentric in the examples and experiences used to illustrate the argument. But in the following year it was translated into Italian, and I was interested to find that this translation aroused very much more discussion in the Italian press than the original version did in England. I was even more surprised that in 1997 the Italian publishers found it necessary to reprint the book, while meanwhile a French edition had appeared in 1993 and a Spanish version in 1996.

I don't think that books like mine have had any effect in changing opinion in Britain. But what has begun this process has been the emergence of direct action anti-road protesters. Other fields of popular protest may be dormant, but proposals for new roads have led to protesting groups digging tunnels or building houses in trees in order to impede the road-building contractors. The young, witty and resourceful protesters, busy impeding the earth-movers, although they are eventually driven out, have begun the process of changing the nation's opinion on new roads.

The book called *Road Raging: Top Tips for Wrecking Roadbuilding*[6] has, I am glad to say, more readers than my modest book, and has been reprinted several times. Young protesters, with nicknames like Animal and Swampy have become heroes of the popular press and

112

television. This is a fortunate trend, and I am convinced that every step we take to replace private transport by community transport will make the environment, whether urban or rural, a more habitable place for the young and the old, and, automatically, for everyone else.

Now I live deep in the country, and since last October, three buses a day have passed our door. They are subsidised by the county council, and when my wife and I get on the bus we tend to be the only passengers on our section of the journey. Our neighbour growls and says, "It should have happened forty years ago." But as we watch down our lane the upgrading of every ancient cottage, 1930s bungalow, barn, farmyard or cowshed, we notice that the first thing to be added is a new, free-standing double garage.

But none of us green-ish folk, if asked where the newest form of radical revolution would appear, would have answered that it would be in obstructing governmental road-building activity. We might very well have quite different priorities. When you talk to the road protesters or to various other rejectors of the organised system, living in travelling settlements, you become aware that they have thoroughly green personalities. They are not conspicuous consumers, but are conspicuously consuming less. Just what we need if we take our green propaganda seriously.

However, we all know that we do not intend to live as they do, and, more importantly, that our fellow-citizens, enjoying lives of conspicuous consumption, regard, not only them, but us frugal folk, with a kind of unbelieving contempt. They will say, like Shakespeare's Sir Toby, "Dost thou think, because thou art virtuous, there shall be no more cakes and ale?"

Our propaganda has to be sharp and subtle, making the culture of Land-Rovers, People-Carriers, Global Cruisers and the rest of the big spending pattern ridiculous, and the do-it-yourself culture alluring and rewarding.

113

Plenty of the building-blocks of the alternatives are well-tried and all around us. In the area of food, you will know all about the attempts in this country to emulate the American Farmers' Markets[7] as well as vegetable box schemes, let alone ancient alternatives like allotments.

In the area of mutual trading and banking you will know about the rediscovery of credit unions and the development of LETS — Local Exchange Trading Systems.[8] You will know better than me about the Leicester LETS and the efforts to establish the Naari LETS in this city.

In the field of housing, I am sure you will know of examples of housing co-operatives as alternatives to both municipal and private landlordism, and about the slow growth of self-build housing endeavours, in particular those associated with the Walter Segal Self-Build Trust,[9] where the most remarkable successes have been among the poorest and most disadvantaged of fellow-citizens. Segal was a delightful freethinking architect and his successors have pursued the greening of housing still further.

In town and country planning there has been a huge ideological step forward with the efforts of the campaign called The Land is Ours. Their doctrine of *Low Impact Development*[10] evolved by Simon Fairlie and published by Jon Carpenter of Oxfordshire stressed three vital questions. They were: "How can there be sustainable development in the countryside under a planning system which explicitly discourages development in the country? How can planners prevent low-income country-dwellers being 'gazumped' by wealthy incomers? and how can we stop the countryside becoming a cross between a factory and a museum?"

It is concern with the practical implications of trying to evolve green attitudes, all these aspects of daily life that seem to me to be characteristics of the green personality. If we cannot defeat the capitalist ideology with its lethal requirement of endless economic growth, then we can at least build alternatives in the spaces in between.

I would be very sorry if I found that green ideologists were creating yet another god called Gaia,[11] some kind of personification of Mother Earth, when there are so many practical green tasks in front of us.[12]

References

[1] Peter Kropotkin: *Fields, Factories and Workshops* (1898, latest edition from Freedom Press, 1984)

[2] Shannon Little: review of *Britain's Share in a Sustainable Future* (Friends of the Earth, 1998) in *New Humanist* December 1998

[3] Nick Davies: *Dark Heart: The Shocking Truth about Hidden Britain* (Vintage Books, 1998)

[4] Alison Ravetz: 'Less costs more for the energy-poor' *Town & Country Planning,* March 1997

[5] Colin Ward: *Freedom to Go; After the Motor Age* (Freedom Press, 1991)

[6] Road Alert: *Road Raging: Top Tips for Wrecking Road-building* (Newbury, 1997)

[7] Harriet Festing: 'So you want to start a farmers' market' *Town & Country Planning,* July 1998

[8] Jonathan Croall: *LETS Act Locally* (Gulbenkian Foundation, 1997)

[9] Walter Segal Self Build Trust, www.segalselfbuild.co.uk.

[10] Simon Fairlie: *Low Impact Development* (Jon Carpenter, 1996)

[11] Gaia — for a free-thinking criticism of making a goddess out of Gaia, see Anthony O'Hear: 'The Myth of Nature' in Barnett and Scruton (eds): *Town and Country* (Jonathan Cape, 1998)

[12] Sustainable lifestyles — for an account of the ideas explored in the lecture, see Ken Worpole (ed): *Richer Futures: fashioning a new politics* (Earthscan, 1999)

Escaping The City

Lecture at the Shelter Conference, York, 18-20 July
1986

Fourteen years ago I was one of a group of people who
were trying to influence the way geography is taught in
the early years of the secondary school through a series of
books called *Human Space* published by Penguin
Education. The idea was to introduce children to
geographical concepts rather than fill them with
topographical information. No sooner were the first three
books rolling off the presses, than ownership of Penguin
changed hands and their education division was closed
down. I had to buy up the remaining copies of my book to
save it from the ignominy of being pulped, and for years I
gave parcels of it to schools and sold copies to adults.

My book was called *Utopia*, since it enquired into
people's ideal places, but it was really about settlement
patterns. In the course of this book I told my readers two
completely true stories about real people. There was the
Quispe family, Quechua-speaking Indians from the
altoplano in Peru, who took the first step of moving,
through hunger, from their village, first to a sugar
plantation on the coast, then to the overcrowded slums of
inner city Lima, and finally to a squatter settlement way
beyond the city limits, where their house and their
economic opportunities grew over time. Then there was
the Byrne family who moved in search of work from Kerry
in the West of Ireland to the city of Cork, and from there
to Canning Town in the London dockland. One August
Bank Holiday they went on an excursion train to Laindon
in Essex and paid a deposit on a six-pound plot of land
where eventually they built a cabin which grew to become
their permanent home after the second world war.

Both families were part of the enormous movements of population in which English cities grew like mushrooms in an incredible expansion of population in the nineteenth century, and in which the cities of Latin America have grown in the second half of the twentieth century. These families of displaced peasants were obliged to throng to the cities and subsequently moved out to the periphery in search of a better life, more space and more opportunities.

Inner-city life was a temporary phenomenon in their family life history, just as it has been in my family life history or yours.

Now of course it is quite wrong to suppose that our cities ever had a golden age. When Britain was the workshop of the world, when the docks were full and when heavy industry was thriving, the newly urbanised city working class was living in poverty and squalor, even when employed. In the last century, when social Darwinism was an acceptable philosophy, observers used to blame the problems of our mushrooming cities on the riff-raff of the population that was immigrating from depressed rural areas. They suggested that the country was exporting its thriftless, footloose elements to the town. At the very same time, observers of what was seen as the crisis of rural life were lamenting that the able, enterprising, stable, bright and adventurous members of the village population were those who emigrated, leaving behind those who lacked these qualities.

A century later it was the cities that were losing population rapidly. The word was spread around in the academic chat shows that this was a disaster, and that the government-sponsored New Towns were to blame, stealing people and jobs from the cities. In vain the advocates of the New Towns pointed out that this planned dispersal had absorbed only an eighth of the enormous outward movement from London, or that of the jobs generated in Milton Keynes, for example, one sixteenth were exported from London. The nineteenth century stereotypes were then brought into play again, but in reverse. The new-found friends of the urban poor claimed that the new towns had taken on only the skilled and enterprising, while teachers and social workers in the New Towns themselves would take me aside and confidentially explain, in the shining new schools, that "we have a terrible lot of problem families with very little motivation and ambition."

All these subjective impressions are relative, of course, and many are based on nothing more than our well-known English snobbery. Ex-urbanite commuters living in towns and villages beyond green belts wouldn't be seen dead in anything so plebeian as a New Town, precisely because the planned new and expanding towns provided housing to rent for people who at the time could not conceivably hope to buy.

It was Stephen Holley, for years the general manager of Washington New Town in County Durham, who summed up the intellectual doublethink of our approach to the loss of population in the cities in the mordant lines:

Isn't it a pity about the Inner City?
People leave who shouldn't ought
And that affects the rate support.
If only those who stayed behind
Had left instead, no-one would mind.

I can remember years ago in 1972 being at a conference in Newcastle, organised by the group called Newcastle Environmental Concern, where the planner Roy Gazzard remarked that on current trends the cities were becoming the habitats of the have-nots and the countryside becoming the habitat of the haves. He prophesied a new fascist elite based on the countryside with its Land Rovers and gadgetry, completely independent of the rest of the population. "Well, that's old Roy," we said, "with his picturesque exaggerations." And of course it *was* a picturesque exaggeration. When, ten years later, Peter Hall came to write the final report of the Social Science Research Council's Inner Cities Working Party, *The Inner City in*

Context,[1] he had to remind us that mistaken prescriptions could result from our stereotypes of the inner city population since, as he put it, "a majority of inner city people are not poor" and since "most of the poor live outside inner cities."

All the same, allowing for the fact that there is a sense in which we can say that only the rich can afford to live in the inner city: others living there on suffrance or through subsidy, there is another sense in which we can perfectly well understand what Maurice Ash, as Chairman of the Town and Country Planning Association meant when he roundly declared that the combination of attempts to shore up the inner cities amounted in practice to nothing less than a conspiracy to *contain* the disadvantaged: "a conspiracy," he said, "because it suits the policies of our centralised state to keep the cities as prisons for the poor. It suits both those who want to manipulate the poor for reasons of power, and those who want to keep them from the preserves of the rich."

Now I'm not talking about the relative merits of urban, suburban or rural life. They have been argued about since at least the time of the Romans. It's a matter of individual or family choice or preference. I say family because those who are free to make a choice usually do so in what they see as the interests of their children. And the choices change at different times in the family life cycle. Metropolitan cities are a magnet for the young and unattached. Some people find them to be fine for the child-rearing part of life. Others don't. Some people think they are great for retirement. Many don't. Above a certain income level there is freedom of choice. Below a certain income level there is no choice at all. And it works both ways. Some people who would like to move to the city can't afford to. Others who would like to move out can't afford to either.

Ebenezer Howard, the inventor of the garden city idea, stressed that the whole purpose of his proposed ring of garden cities was to take the pressure of population off the central city, so that it would be possible to redevelop central areas at those human densities which people sought elsewehere. He was convinced that once the inner city had been "demagnetised" as he put it, once large numbers of people had been convinced that "they can better their conditions in every way by migrating elsewhere," the bubble of the monopoly value of inner city land would burst. It didn't happen that way of course, as every attempt to bring the betterment value of land into the hands of the community that generated it has failed. Howard remarked at a meeting in 1904 that "I venture to suggest that while the age in which we live is the age of the great closely-compacted city, there are already signs, for those who can read them, of a coming change so great and so momentous that the twentieth century will be known as the great exodus, the return to the land."

Well, it may not have been a return to the land but it certainly has been an exodus from the city, and the opportunities for the poor to join in this exodus in search of a more ample life, or because traditional jobs have been evaporating — disappearing into thin air — have steadily diminished. The establishment of Green Belts, with all-party support, has produced what Peter Hall long ago called "a civilised form of apartheid". The rich can buy their way into the green belt, the commuting middle classes can leapfrog it into new settlements and old country towns and villages beyond. This is made clear in a magisterial new study, just published. (*Green Belts; Conflict Mediation in the Urban Fringe* by Martin J. Elson).[2] Professor Lewis Keeble, discussing it in the June 1986 issue of *The Planner*, remarks that this is "the unacceptable face of green belts. How lovely to own a house in an area — town edge, village or green belt — where competition has been removed. Most of the good people who appear at public inquiries to object to development do not, I think, realise that they are supporting gross and unprincipled greed."

In the 1970s the government commissioned a series of Inner Area Studies, and the one called *Inner London, Policies for Dispersal and Balance* by Shankland, Willmott and Jordan (HMSO, 1977) made it perfectly clear that, contrary to the conventional wisdom, excessive population pressure in London "had been *insufficiently* relieved by decentralisation, either planned or unplanned." Yet another new publication from the mountain of research in the inner cities, *The London Employment Problem* by Nick Buck, Ian Gordon and Ken Young, part of the ESRC's Inner Cities Research Programme Series (Oxford, 1986), stresses that "the very selectivity of decentralisation, in which genuine opportunities for movement were available only to those who had access to owner-occupation or who possessed the skills then required in the New and Expanded Towns, had done much to produce this situation."

The Inner Area Study confirmed that there *are* poor people in the inner city who *do* want to get out. All the other evidence identifies the policies that ensure that they can't. The avenues of escape have been closed, one by one.

Thus it wasn't at all fatuous for Mr Michael Salt of Cheshire to write to the *Guardian* on 8th June to say "May I commend the initiative of the 'hippies' in removing their children from the urban wastelands created by the Thatcher government, where they would have been open to the temptations of crime and drugs. These people have endeavoured to teach their children self-reliance and to show them the beauties of the countryside. They practise the epitome of Victorian values... The harassment by the authorities and police; the vilification by the media; and the general nastiness of human nature disgorged upon the poor gives the lie to the notion that freedom exists for any but a privileged class... The saga demonstrates the requirement of a bill of rights for all the citizens of our land."

Well, much as I dislike the government, I don't think the present one created the urban wastelands, nor do I believe in the effectiveness of a Bill of Rights. But his point is underlined by what the members of the convoy* said themselves. Tim Mars, the organiser of this conference, pointed out to me the statements made in interviews with them in Diverse Report on Channel 4 on 11th June:

> Several members interviewed contrasted the convoy way of life explicitly with living in the cities, and described it as a consciously-chosen alternative. They feared that the current harassment and impounding of vehicles is likely to leave them with no choice but to go back to the cities. They talked about a difference in quality of life between being unemployed in the city and unemployed in the community of the convoy. They talked about their right to choose the convoy life and not be forced to live in the city. In choosing mobile accommodation, the convoyers are effectively exploiting the only remaining loophole (thanks to the traditional rights of bona fide gypsies and holiday caravanners) available to people without cash, mortgage creditworthiness or access to new town rented accommodation who nevertheless are determined to escape the city — a loophole which, as we can see, is currently being mercilessly tightened.

There was a time when desperate solutions like that of becoming mobile ruralists in clapped-out old buses, just to get out of the city, would seem absurd. But people do make rational choices from their own standpoint, of the opportunities available to them.

In the first forty years of this century, poor people from inner London, could, like the Byrne family I mentioned earlier, buy a plot of land in South Essex or in Kent, or by the seaside, for a few pounds to put up their shed, shack, shanty or chalet which would start as a holiday retreat, and would grow and be improved over time to become very often, the retirement home of the original builders or the permanent home of their children.

These were the plotlands, in the jargon of town-planners, and you may have attended Dennis Hardy's

---

The general name for the youth sub-culture of New Age Travellers that took to the roads in the 1980s.

lecture about them at last year's Shelter conference. He and I wrote a book *Arcadia for All; the Legacy of a Makeshift Landscape* which is about the plotlanders and is full of detailed case histories.

They were one of the reasons for the all-party support for the strict control of development introduced into post-war planning legislation, and if you read the pre-war literature of planning and conservation you will be made aware of the intense horror that was felt by all right-thinking (that is, privileged) people at the desecration of the landscape they thought they saw. Dean Inge, a famous publicist of the period, coined the phase 'bungaloid growth' with its implication that some kind of cancer was creeping over the face of the Home Counties. Howard Marshall, in the compendium *Britain and the Beast,*[3] declared that "a gimcrack civilisation crawls like a giant slug over the country, leaving a foul trail of slime behind it." In retrospect we can easily see that the greater part of this disgust was ordinary misanthropy. The wrong sort of people were getting a place in the sun.

One of the veterans of the plotlands who talked to us, Mrs Elizabeth Granger, who paid the deposit on her plot in 1932 with a borrowed pound, and since then lived in a number of houses as her family grew, remarked, "We never had a mortgage for any of them. I feel so sorry for young couples these days who don't get the kind of chance we had."

Today we have proposals by Consortium Developments Ltd to construct a new village settlement at Tillingham Hall, in the London Green Belt near Thurrock in Essex. Everyone is watching the result of the appeal, and a great many people for whom the Green Belt was a sacred principle have found that they don't actually want to oppose it. I don't oppose it either. But of course it is totally irrelevant from the point of view of those *poor* city dwellers who want to get out.

---

*The proposals failed and the Consortium was wound up in 1992.

It will be hailed as a disaster or as a breakthrough. Let's seize the opportunity to say that what's good enough for the affluent is good enough for the poor, and that the time has come for a Do-It-Yourself New Town.

If this gives you that eerie feeling that you've been here before, don't worry. You have. I gave a lecture with that title at the Garden Cities/New Towns Forum at Welwyn in October 1975 and repeated it at the ICA in London in February 1976, and got bits of it printed in half a dozen journals as wide apart as *Undercurrents* and the *Municipal Review*. Ten years later, how far have we got? Well, there *have* been the activities of the Greentown group at Milton Keynes and the TCPA's Third Garden City initiative in the form of the Lightmoor project at Telford New Town.

But ten years later I'm even more convinced, from the enormous literature from the Third World, where, as Patrick McAuslan puts it, "the true city builders are the urban poor: their illegal, largely self-built houses are the largest source of new city housing," and from the exhaustive study that Dennis Hardy and I made of the history and evolution of the 'plotlands' of South East England (at the government's expense so far as I was concerned, since I lived for two years on the cash from the Social Science Research Council — every tax-payer has a vested interest in drawing conclusions from our research), I'm even more convinced that if poor city-dwellers had that access to land, security of tenure and access to credit, that is taken absolutely for granted by the better off, they could house themselves by their own action far more effectively and far more cheaply, and with infinitely more dweller-satisfaction, than any outside body could conceivably achieve for them.

Yes, there should be an area where land values are artificially deflated just as they have everywhere been artificially inflated, and where credit and security of tenure are available *and* the planning and building legislation waived. Every experiment in the mildest way which has been proposed, even in Milton Keynes, to let people do what that want just in order to see what happens, has fallen foul of the planners, who want predictions in advance. That's why we need a moratorium on planning. Similarly, compliance with the building regulations demands high standards right from the start. You can't start poor and work your way up to a high standard, which is what every one of our ancestors did in their mud huts, which is what the poor of the Third World are obliged to do, and what the plotlanders did. The building regulations are the biggest current obstacle to anyone doing anything about housing themselves, starting from nothing.

Having been for many years on that circuit of people who dare to advocate that dweller-control is the first principle of housing, I am used to my opinions being misrepresented, so I should add that I am not adding to the various humiliations poor people have to endure the idea that they should be self-builders too. Often they have to be. Often they are good at it. But as any ordinary owner-occupier (and they form the majority of households) knows, there are people round most corners, as well as friends and relations, only too happy to join in the adventure of building, paid in cash or kind, who provide much more satisfaction than the capitalist firms who actually get the council contracts. Nor, since we don't live in an anarchist society, am I letting government off the hook. John Turner put it that "While local control over necessarily diverse personal and local goods and services such as housing is essential, local control depends on personal and local access to resources which only central government can guarantee."[4]

History and geography prove that, given the slightest chance, poor people can house themselves. For a variety of reasons, politicians aren't willing to give them that chance. We can see the diversity of opposition to this in every British city including Liverpool. I'm horrified, of course, but I can't really claim to be surprised.

References

[1] Peter Hall: *The Inner City in Context* (Ashgate, 1981).

[2] Martin J. Elson: *Green Belts: conflict mediation in the urban fringe* (Architecture Press, 1986).

[3] Clough Williams-Ellis: (ed.) *Britain and the Beast* (J.M. Dent, 1937).

[4] John Turner: *Housing by People* (Marion Boyars, 1976).

Is Conservation More than Nostalgia?

Lecture at the Middlesex Polytechnic School of
Geography and Planning, MA Conservation Policy
19 October 1983

In seventy-four days time we will be in 1984, a year which
has been given all kinds of overtones because of George
Orwell's book written in 1948. Publishers never miss an
occasion for a topical book, and I was invited to contribute
to a collection of essays just out called *Nineteen Eighty-
Four in 1984*.[1] My task was to discuss, not the major
themes like the permanent war economy or thought
control, but the minor environmental themes of Orwell's
book, which for this purpose I re-read, for I think the first
time since it came out in 1949. My chapter has the title
"Big Brother Drives a Bulldozer" and one of the themes I
discerned in the text, which I don't remember noticing
over thirty years ago, was that of nostalgia. Let me quote
to you my comments on this theme:

"Nostalgia is one of the great contemporary diseases. It
isn't, as the joke says, what it used to be. It was certainly
never so universal, particularly at the time when
Nineteen Eighty-Four was written. Orwell's friends used
to regard it as a harmless eccentricity that he collected
curious bits of junk and drank his Typhoo tea from a
Victorian commemorative mug. Today, the survivors
among them all, no doubt, have collections of old mugs on
their stripped pine peasant dressers and think them too
precious to drink from. Winston Smith, like his creator,
yearning for a lost past, is hungry for the physical
evidence of the history that has been abolished. He
cherishes the bound album of cream-laid paper that he

bought from a frowsy junk shop in a slummy quarter of town, the place where he later gets scraps of what Orwell calls "beautiful rubbish" like the glass paperweight and the steel engraving of St. Clement's Danes.

"'The world of today,' explains Goldstein in the samizdat book within the novel, 'is a bare, hungry, dilapidated place compared with the world that existed before 1914', (slightly shaky social history of course), 'and still more so if compared with the imaginary future to which the people of that period looked forward. In the early twentieth century, the vision of a future society, unbelievably rich, leisured, orderly and efficient, in a glittering antiseptic world of glass and steel and snow-white concrete — was part of the consciousness of nearly every literate person.'

"Nearly every literate person, faced with the real 1984, hates the cracked glass, rusty steel and stained concrete world and is in the grip of Winston's nostalgia for the world we have lost. Every second-rate building, from the Victorian workhouse to the 1930's factory on the by-pass, has been 'listed' as characteristic of its period (though this never precludes its demolition on a public holiday when there is no-one in the office to receive a complaint). The junk shop is now called 'Things of Yesteryear' or 'Granny's Treasure Box', and the bits of beautiful rubbish have become bygones, if not antiques; even the enamelled advertisements, Bovril jars and ginger beer bottles loved by Orwell are now treasured.

"Winston Smith has a recurring dream of the Golden Country; we turned *The Country Diary of an Edwardian Lady* and *Life in the English Country House* into best-selling books. Even our Prime Minister, a product of the managerial and technocratic rather than the patrician generation, advocates what she regards as Victorian values. What does it mean, this universal nostalgia for a make-believe past? The spread of nostalgia from a foible in 1948 to an obsession in 1984 has several explanations. The most obvious is that we have slowly moved from living in the present to disliking it, and from happily anticipating the future to dreading it."

Well, that's what I said in the Orwell book, and it indicates that a huge component in the conservation movement *is* nostalgia. Since I recognise symptoms of the disease in myself, it isn't for me to disparage it. Politically, it *is* a serious matter. Asa Briggs has just brought out his *Social History of England*, a book consciously intended to replace the famous book by Trevelyan. His final paragraph quotes Ralf Dahrendorf's confession that he finds few things more bewildering about this country than the extent to which public debate is preoccupied with yesterday's world. "It is not likely," comments Briggs, "that this world will survive for long, or that a Conservative government will be primarily concerned with conserving it." I see evidence pointing both ways. On one hand we have the evidence of the Falklands adventure illustrating a nostalgia for an imperial past which, living beyond our means, this country can't afford any more. On the other, in the field of conservation there is every indication that Green Belt policy is going to be sacrificed to the consortium of big building contractors.

In practice we each arrive at some compromise between the claims of conservation and those of some other values. Take this very issue of the Green Belt for example. It makes a lot of difference who is going to build in the Green Belt. I find myself totally opposed to the plans of the consortium of builders while at the same time, I would welcome a relaxation of planning policy towards the self-build enthusiasts or the Greentown Group anxious to find a place in the sun, against the hostility of the well-heeled "We're all right Jack" conservation lobby, the people who want to freeze their particular patch of Our Heritage just as it was on the day before *they* settled there.

Two approaches to conservation which are not the same thing as nostalgia are, first, *historicism* and secondly, *the sense of history*. I distinguish between the two.

Historicism is that view that wants to freeze a place or a building at some particular moment in time. This is the view that wants to take the Victorian plate glass out of a Georgian house and replace copies of the original glazing bars, or that wants to strip off the Georgian façade from a Jacobean house in the High Street, or simply to peel off the rendering from a timber-framed building just to reveal the rough old brickwork between the oak posts.

As you will know, the Society for the Protection of Ancient Buildings has been bedevilled all through its history by the problems presented by historicism. It reprints unaltered in every Annual Report the Manifesto that William Morris wrote in 1877. Morris declared passionately that "of all the Restorations yet undertaken the worst have meant the reckless stripping a building of some of its most interesting material features; while the best have their exact analogy in the Restoration of an old picture, where the partly-perished work of the ancient craftsmaster has been made neat and smooth by the tricky hand of some unoriginal and thoughtless hack of today..." He pleaded that we should "put Protection in the place of Restoration, to stave off decay by daily care, to prop a perilous wall or mend a leaky roof by such means as are obviously meant for support or covering, and show no pretence of other art, and otherwise to resist all tampering with either the fabric or ornament of the building as it stands; if it has become inconvenient for its present use, to raise another building rather than alter or enlarge the old one..."

Well, the Society found this point frequently misinterpreted, and in 1924 added a footnote: "Where there is good reason for adding to an ancient building a modest addition is not opposed to the principles of the Society, provided 1) that the new work is in the natural manner of today, subordinate to the old, and not a reproduction of any past style, 2) that the addition be permanently required and will not in any sense be a building which future events will render inadequate or superfluous."

In other words, Morris and the society he founded were not guilty of historicism, and were willing to tolerate those changes which exemplified the sense of historical continuity, though not for temporary or transitory reasons. Anyone here who has been involved in development control will think of instances where a building has been, as we think, ruined by hacking it about to insert a bit of shop-fitting, while after a couple of years, the shop fails, and the entrepreneur moves on for another attempt to make money, leaving a wrecked building behind him.

My second non-nostalgic motive for conservation is this sense of history, exemplified by two well-known aphorisms or metaphors. W.B. Lethaby remarked that we need old buildings just to prove that the British people had grandparents, and Konrad Smigielski (who was ousted from his job as city planning officer for Leicester on a conservation issue) declared that a town without old buildings is like a man without a memory. The sense of the past (not nostalgia for it) which insists that civilisation and civic or communal life wasn't newly hatched when we ourselves emerged into adulthood, implies a reverence or respect for the labour of others.

I find this beautifully expressed by the German playwright Bertolt Brecht in those poems which celebrate his pleasure in things which bore the marks of long contact with the labour of human hands, his feeling about artefacts. He wrote a famous poem about the objects used as stage props by his wife, the actress Helene Weigel, objects of clay or pewter or worn leather or polished wood; all, he said,

Selected for age, purpose and beauty
By the eyes of the knowing
The hands of the bread-baking, net-weaving
Soup-cooking comprehender
of reality.

There is another poem of Brecht's on a similar theme:

131

Of all works my favourite
Are those which show usage.
The copper vessels with bumps and dented edges
The knives and forks whose wooden handles are
Worn down by many hands: such forms
To me are the noblest. Likewise the flagstones around old houses
Which have been trodden smooth by footsteps, ground away
With tufts of grass between them: those
Are happy achievements.

Taken into use by the many,
Frequently altered, they improve their shape, become special
By general application.
Even fragments of sculpture
With their sliced-off hands are dear to me. They too
Seemed to have lived. They were dropped, and yet they were
  carried.

They were hacked down, yet they never stood too high.
Dilapidated buildings
Again seem half-completed
Enormous projects: their fine proportions
Can already be inferred; yet they still need
Our understanding. At the same time
They have served their purpose, been sloughed off. All this
Delights me.

If you were watching the South Bank Show on television
last Sunday, you saw its account of the work of the
painter John Piper, who confesses his attachment to what
he calls "pleasing decay".

Well, pleasing decay is, by definition, *not* the business
of the conservationist. Quite an interesting discussion
point actually, since W.R. Lethaby, a great architectural
teacher, complained ruefully that the English are in love
with the broken-down picturesque. Piper loathed the way
the ancient monuments people from the Department of
the Environment painstakingly grubbed up the wall-
flowers growing out of the ruined walls.

I am not myself a pleasing decay person. I love
continuity of use. Ten years ago in the book I edited on
vandalism,[3] I urged the reader to imagine some ancient

palazzo in an Italian town. "A dozen families live there, the washing is strung out across the *cortile*, lean chickens and beautiful urchins scratch among the worn flagstones. The massive basement walls at ground level below the *piano nobile* are encrusted with slogans from the last election, with fading messages and peeling posters as well as new pronouncements from the *municipio*. Doesn't he, if he has any feeling for the drama and continuity of urban life, and the needs of the citizens, *prefer* that the building should be used and defaced rather than become a museum, expensively renovated (1955-style) for the benefit of the visiting tourist?"

This, I think, is my own ultimate position on conservation. I love continuity of usefulness in buildings. I like the idea of continuous use and I don't worry all that much about the historical stylistic incongruities that this brings.

I love the *idea* of maintenance: Morris's aim "to stave off decay by daily care". After all, the original meaning of the word "conservation" is simply preservation. "Maintenance" implies understanding and sympathy with the nature of building and the nature of this particular building. There was a much-praised book a few years ago called *Zen and the Art of Motor-cycle Maintenance*.[4] Someone gave it to me for Christmas, and while its philosophical significance was lost on me, I could easily grasp the bit about maintenance. There the narrator implied the contrast between the way he treated his bike, and his understanding of the way an internal combustion engine works — for he was one of those people who can diagnose its malfunctioning just by listening to it and the attitude of his friend who would simply kick his BMW petulantly when it failed to start.

The managerial class, encouraged by the way tax is assessed, assumes that replacement is cheaper than maintenance, and in some ways they are right. They, like the rest of us, laughed at our parents' fixation on hoarding string, because we had all absorbed in the postwar years, the attitudes of affluence which Kenneth Burke described as Borrow, Spend, Waste, Want. Only economic stagnation and reduced incomes make us see the point of an earlier generation's slogan: "Eat it up, Wear it out, Make it do, Or do without." Profligacy, however, is built into our assumptions, and into the way in which revenue is gathered and dispersed. Rural people will know the way this works in the agricultural industry and its effect on rural conservation. But anywhere, as you know, VAT is charged at full rate on maintenance operations in building, but zero-rated on new construction.

Maintenance is not merely a matter of budgetting, it is also a state of mind: a matter of morale and of popular involvement.

Kenneth Campbell, for many years principal housing architect for the Greater London Council, used to say that the decline of the council's estates coincided with the decline of the Royal Navy. How so? Well, all those stokers and chief petty officiers, coming out of the service and needing a flat, would take caretaking jobs, and years afloat had instilled into them the importance of having everything shipshape and maintaining a happy ship. As the supply of such paragons dried up and no-one wanted the job of resident caretaker, the council was obliged to institute its system of mobile caretaking. And the one thing that is inevitable about this depersonalisation of the caretaking function is that a mobile caretaker won't take care.

Visitors to the tenant-controlled public housing in Oslo learned that the secret of the well-tended and trim estates, older than the ones London regards as obsolescent, was that the caretaker held a gold medal for caretaking (and had a budget that enabled him to employ the children of the estate to assist him in his task). In housing, as in industry, and indeed in the environment as a whole, the precondition for shifting us along the sliding scale between slovenly sloth at one end and a self-maintaining system at the other, is to give everyone a vested interest in maintenance.

On the west coast of the United States there sits a longshoreman-philosopher, Eric Hoffer, the author of a couple of useful books about the pitfalls of ideology, *The True Believer* and *The Passionate State of Mind*.[5] Once in a radio interview, he exalted the principle of maintenance to a guarantee of survival. "After the last war," he explained, "when western Europe was in ruins, I thought to myself: If the President should pick me out and send me to Europe to predict which country is going to recover first, I would get the answer in five minutes. I would say: 'Bring me the records of maintenance. The nation with the best maintenance will recover first.' If I should go to Africa and want to tell you which of these 30-some nations is going to be here 50 years from now, I would look around for the rudiments of maintenance. If I got in there in the warehouse, let's say, and I saw that the broom had a special nail, I would say, 'This is the nail of immortality!'"

Ladies and gentlemen, I have given you two motives for conservation: the sense of historical continuity and the instinct of maintenance, which in no way depend on mere nostalgia. I have no doubt that your own discussion will provide others.

References

[1] Paul Chilton and Crispin Aubrey (ed): *Nineteen Eighty-Four in 1984* (Comedia, 1983).
[2] Asa Briggs: *A Social History of England.* (most recent edition Penguin, 1999).
[3] Colin Ward (ed): *Vandalism* (Architectural Press, 1973).
[4] Robert Pirsig: *Zen and the Art of Motor-cycle Maintenance.* (most recent edition Vintage, 1999).
[5] Eric Hoffer: *The True Believer.* (most recent edition Harper, 2009) and *The Passionate State of Mind* (most recent edition Hopewell, 2006).

Colin Ward titles
published by Five Leaves

The Allotment: Its landscape and culture (with David Crouch)*

Talking Anarchy (with David Goodway)*

Arcadia for All: The legacy of a makeshift landscape (with Dennis Hardy)*

Goodnight Campers! The history of the British holiday camp (with Dennis Hardy)

Cotters and Squatters

Remembering Colin Ward 1924–2010 (edited by Ross Bradshaw, Ben Ward, Harriet Ward and Ken Worpole)

---

*currently out of print